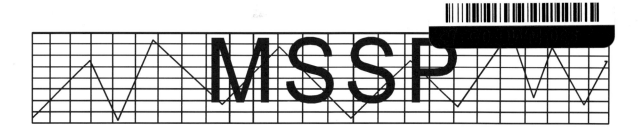

MSSP

Market Segment Specialization Program

Independent Used Car Dealer

 Department of the Treasury
Internal Revenue Service

Training 3147-106 (4/96)
TPDS 84219B

This page intentionally left blank.

TABLE OF CONTENTS

Chapter 4, COST OF GOODS SOLD/INVENTORY

CHAPTER 5, Balance Sheet

Chapter 6, Expense Issues

Chapter 7, Required Filing Checks

Chapter 8, Related Finance Companies

This page intentionally left blank.

Preface

The Independent Used Car Dealer MSSP Guide is a joint effort by the Internal Revenue Service and the National Independent Automobile Dealers Association.

The following have contributed to the development of the Independent Used Car Dealer MSSP Guide:

National Independent Automobile Dealers Association

Internal Revenue Service Jacksonville District

Internal Revenue Service Milwaukee District

Internal Revenue Service Richmond District

Internal Revenue Service Denver District

Motor Vehicle Industry Specialization Program Team

Internal Revenue Service National Office

This page intentionally left blank.

Chapter 1

INDUSTRY BACKGROUND

INTRODUCTION

The used car industry, as with any industry has certain business practices that are used throughout the industry. A key to a successful examination of a used car dealer is an understanding of these basic common practices.

INDUSTRY JARGON

Certain jargon is widely used in the industry. The terms defined in Exhibit 1-1 are the most commonly found terms. However, even these terms may vary from region to region. Nevertheless, the list may be useful in understanding how the industry operates. Become familiar with these terms as many of the terms listed here are used throughout the Audit Technique Guide.

INDUSTRY OVERVIEW

The used car industry is comprised of two major segments. The first segment is made up of the new car dealers who accept trade-ins on the sale of new automobiles; or purchase used cars from customers, used car dealers, or wholesale auto auctions. The new car dealers then sell the used cars either to wholesalers, directly to used car dealers, through auctions, or to other miscellaneous customers.

The second segment of the industry is made up of independent auto dealers; a dealer not affiliated with an auto maker, whose principal business is the sale of used cars. Since no trade franchise (that is, General Motors, Ford, etc.) is necessary, the size of the used car dealer and the capital required to enter the industry varies. However, every dealer must be licensed with the state in which the dealership is physically located. Most states have different laws that govern the ability of individuals or businesses to sell used cars without a license. For example, one state permits an individual to sell up to five cars per year without obtaining a license. Other states are more or less restrictive.

Independent auto dealers acquire cars from trade-ins on the sale of used vehicles, purchase used cars from customers, other new and used car dealers, or wholesale or retail auctions. They may also make private purchase arrangements with individuals who do not purchase a car from the dealer.

Typically, independent dealers maintain one or more sales locations where they keep their inventory. Most of these dealers are engaged in retail sales. For an independent dealer, sales and delivery of the car generally occur on site. The principal source of sales is individual customers, although dealers frequently, for various reasons, sell automobiles to other dealers or through auctions. The retail dealers may also sell cars on consignment.

Wholesalers make up a smaller second segment of the used automobile trade. These dealers do not sell to the general public, and generally do not have a sales lot. A wholesaler buys vehicles from retail dealers and either sells them directly to other retail dealers or takes the cars to auction. They may also purchase vehicles at auction for sale to retail dealers. Some wholesalers also purchase vehicles from public sources such as estates, fleets, businesses, and in response to newspaper ads, etc.

A sales lot used by an independent dealer can generate a significant amount of activity which either produces no sale or is not related to a sales transaction. For example, customers frequently browse just to get an idea of what is available, or may visit the lot several times before buying a car.

Since most independent dealers do not repair customer cars after the customer's purchase, there is normally no service department. However, many dealers maintain a mechanic or have reconditioning facilities to prepare newly acquired vehicles for resale.

Impact of State Regulation and State Law

Every state regulates the operations of the independent dealers, therefore, requirements vary from state to state. Without knowing which state or states are involved, it is impossible to outline what specific requirements are imposed on a dealer. Common dealer transactions that will vary from state to state include:

- Transfers, assignments, and reassignments of titles

- Title transfer processes

- Collection and repossession rights and liabilities

- Consignment rules and procedures

- Payments of commissions for referring buyers

- Documentation for sales and purchases.

Information about the specific state requirements or rules can be obtained from the sources listed at the end of this chapter. Additional information on state laws may be obtained from your state Motor Vehicle Division.

Curbstoners

One problem that the industry faces is the unlicensed dealer (curbstoner) who buys, sells, and trades used cars in excess of the state's licensing requirements without a license. In almost every case, the curbstoner has no fixed place of business and fails to adhere to most of the accepted industry practices or customs. It is not known how much revenue is generated by the curbstoners, although industry officials acknowledge that the amount is significant. **Since the curbstoners operate outside the law, there is a high probability that the income generated by their sales is unreported.**

A state's attempts to enforce the licensing laws against the curbstoners is hampered by lack of personnel and money. Furthermore, with no fixed place of business, it is often difficult to track down a curbstoner. Signs that an individual is curbstoning include:

- Multiple auto listings in a paper with the same phone number

- Displays of multiple vehicles "for sale" in shopping centers or similar parking lots all with the same phone number

- Information obtained from National Auto Data Service (NADS).

Once evidence indicates that an individual or business is engaged in curbstoning, a referral to the appropriate state regulatory agency may be appropriate. **Check with your District Disclosure Office before making any referrals to other agencies.**

Records

The Federal Truth in Mileage Act requires odometer readings to be retained by both the buying and selling dealer. Most states require that a licensed dealer maintain certain records which must be available for inspection by the appropriate state licensing or   regulatory agency. Information about the records a dealer is required to maintain in a particular state can be obtained from the state agency responsible for the regulation of independent dealers. (Normally this will be the state Motor Vehicle Division or the state Department of Revenue.) Aside from these state and federal requirements, other specific records that must be maintained will vary from state to state.

The sophistication of the accounting systems and records will normally vary with the dealer's size and location. However, there are certain common industry practices that provide documentation for a sales transaction. These practices will vary from state to state, since each state has different record requirements, but the basics will be the same. These industry practices are discussed in the various sections on income recognition and inventory. Currently, there is no overall computer accounting program specifically designed for independent dealers, however, there are many programs that are used by dealers.

The key record of a sale is the car jacket, customer file, or deal jacket. A separate file is normally maintained for each sale. Many dealers create a car jacket whenever a car is purchased and assign a stock number to the vehicle. In that case, the car jacket may also be used to track the cost of the car and the cost of reconditioning the car for sale. The file generally contains:

Cash Sale (No Trade-in)

1. Sales order (including the VIN),

2. Buyers name, address and other information,

3. Sales Price,

4. Sales tax (depending on the state, sales tax may be on the gross sales price or net sales price),

5. Doc fees,

6. State and Federal Disclosure statements, including odometer readings,

7. Vehicle stock number,

8. Extended warranty or service contract information and any purchased insurance information,

9. Form 8300, if applicable.

Sales with Trade-ins

1. Same items as for a cash sale,

2. Payoff on any outstanding loans, if applicable,

3. ACV of trade-in.

The customer file may be a separate manila folder, an envelope with the information in it, or simply papers stapled together. All are acceptable methods of record maintenance.

A dealer will normally also maintain a cash receipts record that will show the deposits made by the dealer on a daily basis. An analysis of the deposits will indicate the sources of the dealer's revenues, which could include:

- Auto sales

- Collections on self-financed sales

- Commissions from service/warranty contracts sold

- Commissions from disability and life insurance contracts sold

- Commissions from bank financing.

Consignments

Dealers often sell cars on consignment. In these cases an individual may contract with the dealer to sell the car. The individual receives a stated price upon the actual sale of the car. The dealer receives either a fee or any excess of the sales price over the stated price agreed to with the owner. There are two different practices for recording the cost aspects of the consigned cars.

In the first and preferred method, when the consignment agreement is entered into, a stock number is assigned to the car. Costs incurred in prepping and repairing the consigned car are posted to its assigned stock number. The stock numbers assigned to consigned cars may have a different numbering system or some other designation that quickly identifies the vehicle as a consigned car. At the time of sale, the consigned car is then assigned another stock number to reflect the stated price to be paid the owner, and the reconditioning costs are transferred to the new stock number.

Under the second method, a stock number is not assigned until the sale of the consigned vehicle actually occurs. In either method, incidental and reconditioning costs incurred by the dealer are deducted from the stated price paid to the owner. Many dealers also treat consignment sales from other dealers differently than consignment sales from the general public. Consignment sales from the general public are more detailed in the dealer's books because of titling concerns.

Auctions

One significant source of inventory for dealers is an auction. Dealers use auctions both to buy and sell cars. Dealers use wholesale auctions, where only dealers are permitted to buy or sell. Most dealer transactions are handled by the wholesale auctions. There are also retail auctions which are open to the general public, which may be used by the dealers as well.

Each auction is run independently, maintains different records, and has its own procedures. Some common rules and procedures are used in the auction industry. Standard auction procedures include:

- Every dealer must register with the auction,

- The dealer will provide the auction with the year, make, VIN, and equipment of each vehicle offered for sale, either by phone or on site,

- The auction will issue the selling dealer an auction check, thereby assuming the risk of collection on the buyer's check,

- The auction will handle the actual assignment of title to the buyer,

- The seller may set a floor or lowest price that the car may be sold for by the auction.

Generally, an auction is held once a week. It is common for dealers to attend more than one auction a week since each auction offers different cars for sale. Special manufacturer and fleet auctions are held at various times throughout the year. Dealers often attend several auctions a month, many of which are in another state. By attending auctions outside of his or her area, a dealer is able to take advantage of better market conditions for a specific type of car. For example, a dealer in Florida may want to purchase convertibles, which may have a high price in the Florida market. However, a Wisconsin auction may offer several convertibles for sale at much lower prices due to the lack of a market. The Florida dealer will travel to Wisconsin, buy the convertibles and sell them to customers in Florida. Clearly, the Florida dealer in this example benefitted from another market by attending an auction in another part of the country.

While the overwhelming number of dealers may have a valid business reason for attending out of state auctions, such practices are also a compliance concern. See Travel and Entertainment under Chapter 6, Expenses, for details. A few dealers have been found attending out of state auctions to facilitate buying and selling cars "off the books."

The starting point of an auction is the registration of the dealers participating in the auction, either as buyers or sellers. The auction generally requires that the dealer be registered in advance. This usually involves obtaining a copy of the dealer's license.

Once registered, the dealer may participate in the auction. The selling dealer will provide the auction with the appropriate information about the cars offered for sale, as discussed previously. The cars will be assigned a number, which will be displayed on the windshield, and offered for sale. Since the seller has the right to set a floor price for which the car may be sold, not all cars offered for sale by the auction are sold. However, roughly 60 to 80 percent, on average, of the cars will be sold.

Once the buyer has successfully bid on the car, he or she is afforded an opportunity to inspect the car to be sure that all representations about the car, made by the seller, are correct. If there are no problems, the buyer then proceeds to settlement, and gives the auction his or her check for the purchase price. The auction fills in the title in the buyer's name and delivers the title to the buyer.

On the other side of the transaction, the seller will sign the title and deliver it to the auction for completion. The seller will then receive an auction check, with the restrictions noted below. Each party will also receive an invoice that shows the vehicle sold, as well as the identities of the seller and buyer. The auction invoice will also usually include the executed odometer forms.

The auction will not usually issue payment to a dealer without proof that a business bank account exists. Additionally, the auction normally provides restrictive endorsements on the check issued to the dealer to be certain that the proceeds are deposited to that account. For example, an auction will not issue a check to an individual, but will issue the check in the individual's business name. The check will normally bear some restrictive endorsement on the back, such as "For Deposit to Account of Payee Only." Many auctions request a copy of a dealer's check to verify with the bank that the dealer actually has an account there.

Since the auctions guarantee that the vehicle titles are lien free, the auctions handle all title issues to ensure that the transfer is made correctly. Some common title problems include incorrect VIN's, unsatisfied liens, incorrect title assignments, and an improper chain of title. The auctions have a great deal of experience with interstate transactions and generally have a very good working relationship with the various state Motor Vehicle Divisions.

Titling Issues and Processes

Titling procedures are determined by state law, thus there are 50 different sets of rules that apply. The state Division of Motor Vehicles, or similar agency, regulates the issuance and transfer of a vehicle's title and maintains a record of the owner. This information is available, although its usefulness in tracking an unreported sale or sales will depend on the database used by that particular state. In most states dealer to dealer transfers of title are accomplished through dealer reassignments. These reassignments are not usually recorded unless the state issued the original title or is recording the title once the car is ultimately sold to a retail customer. All of these issues are compounded by the tremendous amount of interstate sales that occur. Although the use of state title transfers do have drawbacks and cannot be used to reconstruct or determine all of a dealer's sales, it remains a useful tool in checking the accuracy of reported sales. Despite no uniformity in titling rules or procedures, some very basic elements exist in all states:

- Every car must have a title,

- There must be a written record of the sales transaction given to a customer,

- A title must contain certain specific information, although the contents will vary from state to state,

- A valid title must be produced at the time of sale, but some exceptions exist for old cars in some states,

- Only dealers can reassign title, individuals cannot reassign titles.

Generally, title to cars purchased at an auction is reassigned directly from the seller to the buyer, although some states require the auction to note on the reassignment of title that the transaction is an auction sale. Some dealers may also purchase cars titled in Canada. Canadian titling laws are much different than those in the United States, and advice on procedures should be sought from an international examiner, who can put you in contact with the Revenue Service Representative. Do the same with any dealer transactions in Mexico.

Dealers need not take actual title to a car, but can reassign the title. This may be done on the title, or on a separate sheet attached to the title. The significance of reassignment is that the dealer will not have to register the title with the Motor Vehicle Division until the car is sold "at retail" to a nondealer customer. This can make tracking the sale of a car very difficult.

Example 1

A dealer in Virginia takes a car with a Maryland title in trade on a sale. The dealer then sells the trade-in at a North Carolina auction, where the title is reassigned to the North Carolina dealer who acquires the car. That dealer then sells the car to a

Florida dealer with a reassignment of title. The Florida dealer then sells the car to a New York dealer, again reassigning the title. Finally, the New York dealer sells the car to a California dealer, by yet another title reassignment. The California dealer then sells the car to a California resident. The new title will be issued by California to the retail purchaser. California may notify Maryland, the state with record of the original title, of the new title. Maryland would then cancel the original title. The notice will show all of the reassignments. However, no title record of the vehicle's sales will appear in any of the intervening states. The Virginia, North Carolina, Florida and New York Motor Vehicle Divisions will not record the car being sold in their state. However, each dealer should have a car jacket or customer file on each car.

Automobile Sales

Used automobiles, obviously, are the principal source of income of a dealer. The sales of autos will generally be made to three broad groups. First, the bulk of the income will be from the sale of a single car to an individual buyer. However, the dealer may also have income from sales to other dealers or wholesalers and from the sale of vehicles at wholesale or retail auctions.

Generally, sales proceeds from an auction will be paid to the dealer by check marked "deposit only" or "deposit only to the account of payee." Payments from sales to other dealers can be in cash, by check or from the proceeds of loans made by a third party. If more than $10,000 is received in cash, the dealer will be required to file Form 8300, Report of Cash Payments over $10,000 Received in a Trade or Business. See the Chapter 7, Required Filing Checks, for more information concerning Form 8300.

The ultimate determination of the sales price will depend on a number of factors. Unlike most retail sales, the sales price of the car is negotiated between the dealer and prospective buyer. The initial "sales price" (asking or list price) established by the dealer is rarely the final sales price. The difference is a discount allowed to the buyer. However, that discount will not be determined the same way for each buyer because each buyer is motivated by different needs and desires. Thus, some buyers want a large discount and accept the dealer's valuation of the trade-in; others want a large trade-in allowance (which in effect reduces the discount the dealer is willing to give) and still others only worry about the monthly payment. Since the dealer is interested in the bottom line profit on the sale of the car, the sales price on substantially the same vehicles may differ greatly. For example, an individual who is willing to accept the ACV for his or her trade-in may have a lower sales price (or greater discount) than an individual who insists on a trade allowance greater than the trade-in's ACV; as illustrated by the following.

1-9

Example 2

A dealer wants a gross profit of $500 each on two identical cars each with a cost basis of $3,000. The asking price of each car is $3,900 before any discounts. Customer #1 has negotiated a final sales price of $3,500, with a $2,000 cash payment and a trade-in allowance of $1,500 which is the ACV of the car traded in. The sales contract may show the net price of $3,500 ($2,000 + $1,500) or the gross price of $3,900, less a discount of $400. Customer #2 has a trade-in with an ACV of $1,500, but refuses to accept anything less than $1,750 for his trade-in. For the second customer, on the identical vehicle, the final net sales price will be $3,750 ($2,000 + $1,750) to take into account the $250 over-allowance.

In each of these cases, the gross profit is $500; however, the sales price and trade allowances are different. Furthermore, in each case, the cost of the trade-in for inventory purposes will be $1,500. The proper accounting entry to record a sale with a trade-in is as follows using the gross sales price (using the example above):

	CUSTOMER 1		CUSTOMER 2	
	DR	CR	DR	CR
Cash	2,000		2,000	
Discount	400		150	
Overallowance			250	
Purchases or	1,500		1,500	
Inventory				
Sales		3,900		3,900

Notice that the only difference between these two transactions is that for Customer #1, the dealer combined the Overallowance and discount into one account, rather than maintain separate accounts for each type of discount. Note that a dealer may also account for the sale as a net sale, in which case the discount and overallowance would be netted against the sales price, and the net figure recorded as the sales price.

Many dealers do sell service or warranty contracts at or close to the time of the sale of the vehicle. These service/warranty contracts are most often third party contracts, with the dealer receiving a commission for the sale. Recently, some dealers have begun to establish separate related companies to sell these contracts.

There are several business reasons to establish a separate company to sell the contracts. Liability can be isolated in a separate entity, ownership of the separate entity can be spread among employees or family members, and any problems associated with the sale of these contracts can be handled without jeopardizing the car sales business. There are no inherent prohibitions against using a separate company for this business, and there are normally no additional costs, above the normal costs of creating a new entity, that are incurred.

INITIAL INTERVIEW

The initial interview is crucial in all examinations. When examining an independent used car dealer, as with all other examinations, the standard interview questions are required. There are a number of specific industry related questions that should also be included as part of the interview process. These questions will help the examiner gain an understanding of how the dealer operates his or her business and help determine the scope and depth of the examination. **Remember to be flexible and adapt the line of questioning to the taxpayer's responses.**

During the initial interview, the examiner should address the dealer's internal controls. Areas to consider include what the owner is doing to protect himself or herself from the occasional dishonest employee. This is of primary concern when examining buy here/pay here lots where customers are coming in with weekly payments on financed cars. The need for the determination of whether internal controls are adequate increases when the owner or close relatives are not physically present on the business premises or if the taxpayer has more than one business. When questioning the owner on how cash is handled, the examiner should appraise the responses in light of whether they are likely to protect the owner. Effective questioning may lead to the identification of records that would not have been provided during the course of the examination. For example, the examiner may want to ask the owner if he or she keeps a personal record or list of his or her profits on each vehicle or deal. The examiner may also want to ask what other records, listings or summaries on business transactions other than those already provided the business or owner maintained.

General Questions

1. What types of sales transactions did you have for the year under examination?

    a. Any sales at auctions? If yes, which?

    b. Any sales to wholesalers? If yes, which?

    c. Any sales to other dealers? If yes, which?

    d. Any consignment sales? If yes, volume?

    e. Any scrap sales? If yes, describe.

f. Any in house dealer financing sales?

g. Any third party financing sales?

h. Did you have any other types of sales transactions?

i. Did you have any sales that resulted in a loss on the sale? If yes, describe the nature of these sales.

j. What sales did you have to relatives or family friends during the year? Identify.

2. Besides the above sales transactions, what are your other sources of income or revenue?

a. Interest income on dealer financed sales?

b. Commissions or referral fees on third party financing?

   1) What third party financiers did you primarily use?

   2) What was the fee/commission arrangement?

c. Commissions or referral fees on car insurance placement?

   1) Which insurance companies were primarily used?

   2) What was the fee/commission arrangement?

d. Commissions or referral fees on warranty/repair placement programs?

   1) Which were used?

   2) What was the fee/commission arrangement?

e. What other commission/referral fee arrangements do you have income from?

f. What other sources of income/revenue do you have?

g. Do you have any other sources of income/revenue that we have not discussed? If so, please describe.

How Sales Are Recorded

1. When selling a vehicle, how do you report the sale?

   a. Gross sales price per Sales Contract?

   b. Net cash received upon sale after discount and/or trade-in?

2. Through the use of a sales contract transacted in the year under examination, show me how you recorded the sale.

3. Do you have an outside accountant/bookkeeper record your sales? If so, explain in detail what records you provide.

4. Are sales taxes reported in the gross sales price?

5. Are licensing fees or titling fees included in the sales price? (Note; if answer is no, look for them as expense items, if so, make the appropriate adjustment.)

6. If the sales taxes and/or licensing and titling fees are reported in gross sales, how do you account for them? Are they listed as a separate item on the books?

7. How often do you reconcile deposits to income? Identify the specific bank accounts that sales are deposited to.

8. Give specific examples of when sales have not been deposited.

9. Have you ever deposited any sales receipts into any other bank accounts (payroll account, personal draw account, etc.)? If so, list them.

10. Explain how cash sales transactions are recorded.

11. Do you have any business expenses in which you pay cash? Provide specific examples.

12. How do you access the cash for these expenses? What is the original source of these cash funds?

13. How do you treat customer deposits?

    a. How are they recorded on the books when received?

    b. How are they recorded when the sale is finalized?

14. Do you have a minimum deal gross profit percentage or dollar amount ($100 minimum profit, etc. per car) for consummated sales?

    a. Do you disregard your minimum gross profit to consummate a sale?

    b. Do you use an average gross profit markup in establishing the original sales price for the year under examination?

    c. NOTE: If used, the average gross profit markup for a car that is common, in average condition, and in a common color will reflect a gross profit significantly different than that of a car in limited supply.

15. Do you sell warranty programs?

    a. How do you record the income from them on the books?

    b. How do you record the expense items on the books?

    c. Note: Be attentive to proper timing of income/expenses.

16. Do you finance sales?

    a. How do you record the income from the financing on the books?

    b. Note: Be attentive to proper timing of income.

17. Do you sell finance contracts?

    a. How does this transaction work?

    b. Who do you sell finance contracts to?

    c. Have the taxpayer walk you through a specific example.

    d. Do you own or are you a shareholder of the finance company?

    e. If the owner of the car dealer is also an owner of the finance company, see Related Finance Companies under Accounting Methods for additional information.

    f. Do you have a dealer reserve account at any financial institution? (See discussion of finance reserve income (Commissioner v. Hansen, 360 U.S. 446 (1959)) in the Gross Receipts section of this ATG.)

18. What other goods or services do you provide in your business? How are these transactions reported on the books? Car repairs? Portering/detailing services? Car mats, etc.?

Pricing Policies and Discounts

1. When setting an asking price for a vehicle, what information sources do you consult, for example, Blue Book?

2. When valuing a trade-in vehicle, what method do you use, that is, resale value to a customer, wholesale value to another dealer, or some other method such as personal judgement? Please explain the method by giving an example?

3. How do you arrive at the amount of discount you recognize on a sale? Please provide an example.

4. When overvaluing a trade-in how do you record it on the books? How do your record this paper loss?

5. When recording a sale of a trade-in on the books, how are the ACV and the discount recorded on the books?

Inventory Items

1. When setting an inventory value for a vehicle, what information sources do you consult, that is, Blue Book?

   a. Do you ever change this value?

   b. How is this change in value recorded on the books?

   c. What factors are considered when changing the inventory value?

   d. Do you consistently use one official valuation guide or do you consult more than one? Please explain. (Methods of fixing values differ among valuation guides. See Discussion of Treas. Reg. section 1.446-1(a)(2) in Chapter 4.)

   e. For any vehicle that is valued below cost, how does the asking price at any point in time differ from the value recorded on the books at year-end? Please explain. (The propriety of a write-down may be determined by actual sales price. See discussion on Treas. Reg. section 1.471-4(b) in Chapter 4.)

2. If a car is portered or repairs are made to it for resale, how do you record these costs?

   a. Current expense?

   b. Added to the value of the vehicle?

3. When junking a vehicle for scrap, how do you account for it?

   a. What value is used for vehicles in ending inventory?

   b. Does this value differ from the originally recorded at the time of acquisition?

   c. In determining the yearly LIFO index, what is the vehicle in ending inventory compared to in the ending inventory of the preceding year (that is, the taxpayer's own cost for the same type of vehicle or a "reconstructed" cost from an official valuation guide for the same type of vehicle at the beginning of the year)?

   d. Explain how these vehicles are comparable.

Miscellaneous

1. Have you ever taken items other than vehicles in-trade?

   a. Please explain.

   b. How was this accounted for on the books?

2. Explain the titling regulations that you are responsible for as a licensed car dealer.

3. Provide your log/record of titles for all vehicles sold for the year.

4. Do you acquire vehicles at auctions?

   a. If yes, which auctions?

   b. Which, if any are out of state?

5. Do you acquire vehicles from wholesalers?

   a. If yes, and a few are used, which wholesalers are used.

   b. If yes, and several are used, who are the primary wholesalers?

   c. What out of town wholesalers do you use?

6. What other non trade-in sources of vehicles do you utilize?

   a. What business names do they operate under?

   b. Are any of these businesses out of state?

   c. If yes, which ones are out of state?

7. How can I identify how a vehicle was acquired for resale?

8. How do you gauge the used car market at any given time?

9. How does this affect your pricing and valuation practices?

10. Do you and your family members own a car?

    a. Do you or your family members drive cars off the lot?

    b. If so, which cars are used by you and your family?

    c. How are gas, oil, and other expenses paid and by whom?

    d. Are the use of the car and/or payment of personal car expenses included in income?

    e. If you use a car for business, what records do you keep?

    f. What are the nature of the business trips?

INFORMATION SOURCES ON USED CAR DEALERS

National Independent Auto Dealers Association (NIADA)
2521 Brown Blvd. Ste. 100
Arlington, TX 76006-5299

State Division of Motor Vehicles
(See local phone directory or state government listing for address)

American Association of Motor Vehicles Administrators
4200 Wilson Blvd. Ste 1100
Arlington, VA 22203

National Auto Data Service (NADS)
4211 S.E. International Way
Milwaukee, OR 97222

State Independent Auto Dealers Association
(address can be obtained from NIADA)

State Business Licensing Bureau
(See local phone directory or state government listing for address)

Municipal or County Business Licensing Bureau
(See local phone directory or municipal or county government listing for address)

Financial information on used car retailers and wholesalers, including average financial ratios is available from:

Robert Morris Associates
One Liberty Place
Philadelphia, PA 19103

The Robert Morris business ratios are available at most public or university libraries.

The data in the ROBERT MORRIS ASSOCIATES ANNUAL STATEMENT STUDIES was compiled with the help of commercial bankers. Data generated is useful in giving general information about industries, including used car dealers. The publishers do warn the users that since the averages were not generated from a statistical sample, they should not be used as industry norms. The numbers are, however, very useful for comparative purpose.

Data available includes current year and historical year data (the 4 immediately preceding years) for balance sheet and income statement items. A variety of additional financial ratios are provided.

The data is further broken down by asset size for the current year. Asset and liability classifications closely approximate the balance sheet on a tax return. The income data is sparse, including only three expense classes; cost of sales, operating expenses, and all other expenses.

This page intentionally left blank.

Industry Jargon

A.A.M.V.A. -American Association of Motor Vehicle Administrators. The association consists of the various state motor vehicle department administrators.

ACV - ACTUAL CASH VALUE - The wholesale value assigned to a trade-in or purchase. The ACV will usually differ from trade-in allowance (the credit allowed customer on purchase of car). ACV becomes cost adjusted by reconditioning costs and other costs. The ACV is determined by the dealer at the time of purchase or trade, based on valuation guides and adjusted for the specifics of each vehicle. ACV can be higher or lower than the trade-in allowance.

AUTO AUCTION - Auto auctions are generally of two types. Dealer Auctions are open to licensed car dealers only. Public auctions are open to every one. Selling prices are set through competitive bidding on each vehicle rather than by the seller.

BIRD DOG FEES - A fee paid for a customer referral. The referral may be made by a licensed or unlicensed individual and may be regulated or unregulated by the particular state.

BLACK BOOK - One of several publications listing wholesale and retail price ranges of used cars. See guidebook below.

BOOK VALUE - The wholesale value of a given used vehicle in a specific market area at a particular time of the year, as determined by a recognized wholesale appraisal guide book.

BROKER - A middleman who locates cars for other dealers, usually on a commission basis. A broker does not take title or possession of the cars, whereas a wholesaler takes possession and title of the cars.

BUY HERE/PAY HERE - A dealer that offers in-house dealer financing for the cars sold. (Dealer provides financing either on his or her own or through a separate finance company owned and run by the dealer. Usually the finance company will share employees and office space with the dealership.) Also see Related Finance Company.

CAR JACKET (DEAL JACKET) - The complete history of a vehicle from the time it is purchased to its sale. The jacket should contain, in addition to the purchase and sale price, any invoices and costs associated with repairs, delivery and parts. It also contains any Federal Trade Commission and state required notices such as odometer statements, Vehicle Identification Number (VIN), stock number and records of the sales transaction. The jacket is normally a folder containing all the information, however, some dealers may maintain a ledger sheet or index card on each vehicle instead of the folder.

CHARGE BACK - A loan financed through the dealer is paid off sooner than the loan term. The finance company will make the dealer pay back part of the commission. This also happens with insurance commissions.

CURBING - Sale of a vehicle by an unlicensed dealer from a shopping center parking lot or similar area. See CURBSTONER.

CURBSTONER - An unlicensed dealer. These "merchants" sell in violation of the law, usually from shopping center parking lots or similar areas. Since each state has different licensing requirements, the definition of a "curbstoner" will vary from state to state.

CUSTOMER FILE - Refer to CAR JACKET.

DEAL - The completed sale of a car or truck to an individual or another dealer.

DEALSHEET - The sales order or invoice showing the sale of a vehicle to an individual or another dealer.

DELIVERY EXPENSE - Transportation of used cars from the point of purchase to the dealership, or the cost incurred to transport autos involved in a dealer trade. This activity may also be referred to as hiking or shuttling. The service may be done by the owner, a towing service, self-employed individuals, or employees. This expense may lead to an employment tax issue depending on facts and circumstances.

DETAILING - To prepare a car for resale. This usually includes cleaning, minor repairs and cosmetic work. Detailing is often used synonymously with reconditioning. This may be done by the dealer, an outside business, or individuals brought in to do the work. Also called portering. This expense may lead to an employment tax issue.

DISCOUNT - The difference between the asking or list price established by the dealer and the final sales price of a vehicle.

DOC FEE - A fee charged for processing or handling the documentation of a sales transaction. May also be called procurement fee or processing fee.

DOMEBOOK^(TM) - A journal used by small businesses to help organize income and expenses on a monthly basis. It has separate monthly pages for receipts, purchases, and other expenses.

DOUBLE DIP - Person with a loan for the purchase of a car and with additional outside financing for down payment that may or may not be shown as a lien on the title.

FLOORING/FLOOR PLANNING - Costs incurred in obtaining inventory, usually through loans from a bank or other financial institution. Includes interest on the loans. Some dealers may be utilizing auction floor plans for the purchase of vehicles. This is a growing industry and one that will probably become common in the next few years.

GUIDEBOOK - A book used to value trade-ins and cars in inventory. It is also used for sale purposes. The most common guidebooks used in the industry include the Kelley Blue Book, NADA Used Car Guide, "Black Book," "Red Book," "Gold Book," CPI Book, and Galves. There are other publications that may be used on a regional basis. Guidebooks are often referred to as the Black Book, Blue Book, Yellow or Gold Book. Each of these publications is recognized by the industry as one of the official used car guides for determining values of used cars. The popularity of a particular book varies by region.

HIKING - See Delivery Expense above.

IN-HOUSE FINANCING - Financing provided by the dealer. Also known as Buy Here/Pay Here.

KELLEY BLUE BOOK - One of several publications listing wholesale and retail price ranges of used cars. See guidebook above.

L O C - Line of Credit, usually from a bank. A loan on which the dealer can take out money whenever needed; similar to a checking account with interest charged. The line has a maximum amount that can be outstanding at any time. Similar to floor planning, but not used solely for purchases of inventory.

N.A.A.A. - National Auto Auction Association

N.A.D.A. - National Automobile Dealers Association

N.A.D.S. - National Auto Data Service

NET SALES PRICE - Sales price less any trade-in allowance or discounts.

N.I.A.D.A. - National Independent Automobile Dealers Association.

ONE PAY - Single payment contract for delivery of vehicle. Allows dealer to deliver car to customer immediately rather than waiting for loan approval. Customer usually is obtaining own financing and will pay the sales price in full once financing is provided by the lender. This is often reflected by a demand note from the customer.

OPEN TITLE - A title signed by the seller that has the buyer's name left open or blank. Also called a skip title. Generally, transferring a car with an open title is illegal.

OVERALLOWANCE - The excess of trade-in allowed over the auto's ACV. This is used as a means to close the deal. Usually, the difference is made up by decreasing the discount on the car purchased.

PACKAGE DEAL - The purchase of two or more vehicles for a lump sum price. This generally occurs between dealers and is one way to sell a car that otherwise would be difficult to move.

PORTERING - See DETAILING above.

RATE SPREAD - A rate spread occurs when a dealership had made arrangements to write car loans for a financial institution. The dealership will pre-arrange the amount of interest rate that the financial institution will charge on car loans to buyers. The dealership will then write loans at a higher rate and receive the excess interest generated by the loan as an income payment from the financial institution.

REASSIGNED TITLE - A title transferred from dealer to dealer which may not require processing by the state in which the dealer operates.

RECONDITIONING - Any work done to prepare a vehicle for sale. Includes parts, labor, cleaning, and other work done on a vehicle. May be part of detailing or portering expense.

RELATED FINANCE COMPANY (RFC) - A finance company owned and operated by the dealer. Shows up as a separate entity for tax purposes.

REPO - Repossession of a vehicle when the purchaser defaults on the loan.

SHUTTLING - See DELIVERY EXPENSE above.

SKIP - Renege on payment of a loan. The term also applies to a buyer who can't be located, that is, took off in the middle of the night for parts unknown.

SLED - A vehicle with an actual cash value (ACV) of $300 or less. Also known as a clunker, iron, roach, or pot.

SPIFF - A cash incentive paid to salesmen for selling a special vehicle, such as one that has been on the lot for a long time.

SUBLET - To have work performed by outside vendors, usually when the dealer either is not equipped for the work, or is unable to perform the work within a reasonable time.

TRADE-DOWN - A retail customer trades a car for one of lesser value. Will be found only with retail deals.

TRADE-IN - An item taken in by a dealer as part of a deal on the sale of a vehicle from the dealer's inventory. Usually another vehicle, but may be a boat, motorcycle, camping trailer or other items agreed on by the dealer and customer. Value of the item is deducted from the amount due on the sale of the vehicle purchased.

UNWIND - Reversing a sale due to purchaser's inadequate credit.

UPSIDE DOWN - A sales situation where the trade-in has an ACV less than the remaining loan amount on the car.

USED CAR LOG - A record of all purchases of and sales of used cars, usually showing the year, make, identification number, date purchased, date sold, who it was purchased from and who it was sold to. Requirements will vary from state to state. This book may be referred to as a Police Book or State Log in some parts of the country.

VEHICLE IDENTIFICATION NUMBER (VIN) - The unique identification number assigned to a vehicle by the manufacturer. The VIN is used to specifically identify which vehicle is being sold or traded.

WARRANTY - Protection plan or guarantee on the car and/or certain systems such as the drive train. Length of warranty varies from dealer to dealer.

WASHOUT - A series of sales transactions where the trade-in of a prior sale is sold partially in exchange for another trade-in. For example, Car A is sold for cash plus trade-in of Car B. Car B is then sold for cash and the trade-in of Car C.

WHOLESALER - Specializes in selling vehicles to other dealers for an agreed price. Unlike a broker, the wholesaler takes possession and title of the vehicle. They do not sell to the general public. These transactions may be subject to state and local sales taxes depending of your state requirements. Retail dealers also will sell wholesale to other dealers.

YOYO - A sales situation where the buyer takes the car home subject to financing approval. When the financing is not approved, the customer must return the car.

Chapter 2

ACCOUNTING METHODS

GENERAL INFORMATION

Most used car dealers do not have the sophisticated books and records found at new car dealerships. Internal controls often can be poor at best; and may be totally nonexistent. Records are usually kept by the owner or family member, with the accountant preparing the general ledger from check stubs and deposit slips provided by the owner. In such businesses, it is necessary to closely examine the method of accounting used in preparing the tax returns. Frequently the return will indicate the accrual method of accounting is being used, but further examination reveals either the cash method or installment method of accounting is actually being used.

Used car dealers normally maintain an inventory, which is a material income producing item. Material income producing items are required to be accounted for under an accrual method of accounting. Nationwide, many used car dealers have been found to be using an improper accounting method, either the cash method or the installment method.

In parts of the country, dealers will report inventory under the accrual method, but account for sales under the installment method. This improper method is evident when an auto is purchased from the dealer under an installment plan. Instead of reporting the full sales price as income at the time of the sale, income is reported ratably over the life of the installment plan. This improper method defers the reporting of income to subsequent years for installment plans that overlap tax years.

Hybrid accounting methods are frequently used by used car dealers. The most common hybrid method involves using the accrual method for gross receipts and cost of goods sold and the cash method for other expense items. Such methods are acceptable as long as they clearly reflect the dealer's income and conform to the regulations.

Dealers may have more than one business operating at the same location. Provided requirements are met, those other businesses may be eligible to use the cash method of accounting. The method is acceptable as long as it clearly reflects the dealer's income from the business and conforms to the regulations. The car dealership and the other businesses should be on separate returns or Schedules C.

It is important to note that Internal Revenue Code section 448 does not affect the authority of the Internal Revenue Service to require the use of an accounting method that clearly reflects income or the requirement that the taxpayer secure the consent of the Internal Revenue Service prior to changing its accounting method (Temporary Treasury Regulation section 1.448-1T(c)). For example, a taxpayer may be required to change its accounting method under IRC section 446(b) to the accrual method because it more clearly reflects income.

A method of accounting involves the consistent treatment of a material item. A material item is any item that involves the proper time for the inclusion of the item in income or the taking of a deduction (Treas. Reg. section 1.446-1(e)(2)(ii) and Rev. Proc. 91-31, 1991-1 C.B. 566). Section 2.02 of Revenue Procedure 92-20, 1992-1 C.B. 685, provides a definition of "method of accounting." It states in part: "the relevant question is generally whether the practice permanently changes the amount of taxable income." Consistent treatment is established by using an improper method for 2 or more tax years (Rev. Proc. 92-20, 1992-1 C.B. 685 and Rev. Rul. 90-38, 1990-1 C.B. 57) and a proper method for one year (Treas. Reg section 1.446-1(e)(1)).

CHANGE OF ACCOUNTING

Treas. Reg. section 1.446-1(e)(2)(ii) defines a change in method of accounting as a change in the overall plan of accounting for gross income or deductions, or a change in the treatment of any material item. An accounting method change will invariably cause timing differences in reporting of income or deductions.

Generally, there are two adjustments necessary for a change in method of accounting. The first will require an adjustment to income in the year of change to avoid duplication or omission of income or deductions under IRC section 481(a). This adjustment is the timing difference between using the old method of accounting and the new method of accounting. The adjustment may consist of adding to income:

1. items not previously reported as income, such as accounts receivable, and

2. items previously deducted, such as any beginning inventory; or deducting from income items not previously deducted, such as accounts payable.

These adjustments are determined as of the beginning of the year of change. A second adjustment under IRC section 446(b) accounts for the difference in taxable income determined under the new method of account for the year of change as compared to the old method.

Rev. Proc. 92-20 provides the administrative procedures applicable to changes in methods of accounting. It applies a gradation of incentives to encourage voluntary compliance with proper tax accounting principles, and to discourage taxpayers from delaying the filing of applications for permission to change an improper accounting.

There are two principle types of methods of accounting: Category A methods and Category B methods. A "Category A" method is any method that is specifically not permitted to be used by the taxpayer by the Internal Revenue Code, regulations, or by a decision of the U.S. Supreme Court. A "Category A" is also any method that differs from a method the taxpayer is specifically required to use under the Internal Revenue Code, regulations or a decision of the U.S. Supreme Court. If a method of accounting is "specifically not permitted," it is a Category A method, regardless of whether the method is acceptable under GAAP. For example, inventory write-downs in Thor Power Tool Co. v. Commissioner, 439 U.S. 522 (1979), are acceptable under GAAP, but not for federal income tax purposes. Since Thor Power was a Supreme Court decision, the use of such write-downs in valuing inventory is a Category A method of accounting. A Category B method is any method that is not a Category A method.

Rev. Proc. 92-20 allows a taxpayer under examination to apply for a change in method of accounting during the 90-day period beginning on the day after the beginning of the examination. If the present method of accounting is a Category A method, a positive adjustment in this year of change is the first year of the examination and the IRC section 481a) adjustment is spread over 3 years. If the present method of accounting is a Category B method, a positive adjustment in this year of change is the "current" year, and the IRC section 481(a) adjustment is included in full in the year of change, that is, no spread.

A negative IRC section 481(a) adjustment, resulting from a Category A accounting method change and applied for within the 90-day window, is taken into account in one year (the year of change). A negative IRC section 481 adjustment, resulting from a Category B accounting method change, is taken into account ratably over 6 years or less. See section 6.02(2)(b) and (3)(b) of Rev. Proc. 92-20, 1992-1 C.B. 685, 693.

The year of change with regard to both Category A and Category B adjustments may differ based upon whether the adjustment is positive or negative. For example, the year of change in the case of a Category A positive adjustment (that is, the earliest taxable year under examination or, the first taxable year under examination the method is considered impermissible) is different from the year of change in the case of a Category A negative adjustment (that is, the taxable year for which a Form 3115 filed as of the first day of the 90-day window would be considered timely filed under the rules for a taxpayer not under examination). See section 6.02(2)(a) of Rev. Proc. 92-20.

Different rules apply to all LIFO method changes.

Issue

Is the proper accounting method being used?

Audit Techniques

1. Ask the taxpayer or representative how sales were recorded and if any credit sales were made.

2. Review the sales journal for recurring payments from individuals.

3. If detailed sales journals are not available, review deposit slips for recurring payments from individuals. This may indicate the dealer is on a cash or installment basis for reporting income.

4. Review sales invoices for terms of sales.

5. If the taxpayer is using either the cash or installment method of reporting income, you will need to determine the amount that has not been reported as income for the remainder of the life of the contract. This can be done in one of two ways:

    a. Use the accounts receivable balances at the end of the year to determine the unreported income resulting from the improper accounting method; or

    b. Analyze the sales contracts to determine which contracts have not been fully reported as income in the year under examination and subsequent years.

6. Determine whether the dealer offers in-house financing, and if so, whether all income from the sale is included at the time of the sale. See the section on financing for details on handling this issue.

References

IRC section 446(c) lists the permissible methods of accounting for computing taxable income.

IRC section 448 places limits on the use of the cash method of accounting.

IRC section 453(b)(2)(A) and (B) disallow the use of installment method on any dealer disposition and disposition of personal property that would have to be included in inventory if the property were on hand at the close of the taxable year.

IRC section 481 sets forth rules for adjusting income for the year of change when there is a change in the method of accounting and for calculating the tax by limiting the tax to an amount of the tax that would result from allocating the increase to income from the change to the year of change and the preceding 2 years.

Treas. Reg. section 1.446-1(c)(2)(i) states that in any case in which it is necessary to use an inventory, the accrual method of accounting must be used with regard to purchases and sales unless otherwise authorized under subdivision (ii) of the subparagraph.

Wilkinson-Beane, Inc., v. Commissioner, 420 F.2d 352 (1st Cir. 1970). The Court of Appeals upheld the decision of the Tax Court that the Commissioner was justified in changing the accounting method to the accrual basis to reflect income. The fact that the difference between the cash and accrual method was less than two tenths of one percent was immaterial.

Smith v. Commissioner, T. C. Memo. 1983-472. The court ruled that where the purchase and sale of automobiles was the principal income-producing factor in a used car dealer's business, requiring the use of an inventory, the dealer was required to use the accrual method of accounting.

Rev. Proc. 92-20, 1992-1 C.B. 685, provides the general procedures for obtaining the consent of the Commissioner to change an accounting method under Treas. Reg. section 1.446-1(e). Section 6 provides procedures for taxpayers under examination.

Rev. Proc. 92-74, 1992-2 C.B. 442, provides the procedures by which certain taxpayers required to use inventories to clearly reflect income may obtain expeditious consent to change their accounting method to either:

1. An overall accrual method, or

2. An accrual method in conjunction with a request to change to a special method.

This Revenue Procedure modifies and supersedes Revenue Procedure 85-36, 1985-2 C.B. 434.

This page intentionally left blank.

Chapter 3

GROSS RECEIPTS

INTRODUCTION TO GROSS RECEIPTS

The majority of a used car dealer's income will come from the sale of cars. Not all car sales are retail sales. Dealers can and do sell to other dealers, often in package deals. Dealers may also sell vehicles at various auctions, both wholesale (dealers only) and retail (public) auctions. Since inventory is a significant part of a dealer's business, the dealers are required to use the accrual method of accounting for sales and cost of sales. However, where permission has been obtained, some hybrid methods of accounting may be appropriate for other expense items. For a detailed discussion of appropriate accounting methods, see the Chapter 2.

Many dealers will accept cash payments in addition to personal checks, money orders, and bank drafts. Dealers receiving cash or cash equivalents in excess of $10,000 are required to file Form 8300 with the IRS. See the Chapter 7, Required Filing Checks, for a detailed discussion of Form 8300 requirements.

Throughout the country, a number of dealers have been found to be recording sales at net rather than gross and showing the amount of the trade-in as a return or allowance on the sales contract. They then take the sale of the vehicle they received in trade and include it as cost of goods sold when it is sold. This treatment results in a double deduction of the cost of an auto taken as a trade-in.

It is necessary that the examiner establish and understand the dealer's handling of a vehicle for gross receipts, purchases, inventory, repossessions, and trade-ins. Only when the examiner understands the dealer's accounting for a vehicle from the time it is acquired to the ultimate sale, can the examiner:

1. Choose and tailor the audit techniques best suited for the dealer, based on the records and accounting procedures used, and

2. Ensure that income and costs are not being omitted or duplicated by virtue of the dealer's accounting procedures.

INTERNAL CONTROLS

Many used car dealers tend to have poor internal controls; therefore, gross receipts must be examined closely. Poor internal controls can be found in both sole proprietorship and corporate businesses. The owner/shareholder or family members will make the bank deposits and keep the records of cash receipts and sales. Often records of the cash receipts, based on these bank deposits, are given to the accountant as the monthly sales figures. The bank deposits are reconciled by the accountant and these figures may be used as gross receipts on the return.

MISCELLANEOUS INCOME

In addition to the sale of used cars, many dealers have secondary and related sources of income. These include:

- Service contract income

- Financing income

- Insurance income.

Not all dealers have all of these secondary sources of income, but it is common for a dealer to have one or more of these sources of income. Generally, these secondary sources of income will be listed on the customer file.

Used car dealers may also provide other services. These services that generate other sources of income include body repair work and routine maintenance such as oil changes and tune ups. Leasing used cars on plans similar to those of the new car dealers has become another popular source of income in certain parts of the country.

Dealers may also buy vehicles that are later scrapped or junked. Where this occurs, it is common for parts from the car to be used to recondition other cars that are eventually sold to customers. A dealer may also buy cars that are already scrap cars (also called junked cars) for parts that are used to recondition cars for sale to customers. The parts taken from a junked car may be used to recondition several cars (for example, the carburetor used for one car, the alternator used for another, etc.). However, it would be unusual for the parts to be sold to third parties, since there is no network for such parts. A proportionate cost of the parts used should be added to the inventoried cost of the car sold. Once the usable parts have been removed, the junked car is normally sold to a scrap or junk yard for a small fee. The income received from the scrap or junk value of the car should be recorded on the dealer's books, although it is usually very small, normally under $50 per car. Not many dealers regularly get involved in the purchase of scrapped or junked cars due to space limitations and the appearance that the cars present on the dealer's lot.

Dealers will frequently attend auctions to purchase cars for inventory. Many auctions give prizes with the purchase of certain cars, or hold drawings for prizes during the auction. Frequently these prizes may be of minimal value, however, large items such as television sets and stereo equipment may occasionally given away. Such prizes are includible as income to the owner of the dealership. New car dealers may also give prizes to used car dealers for purchasing certain cars or a number of cars during a certain period of time.

Fee Income

Auction fees are payments collected by a dealer for purchasing a particular vehicle for a customer at auction. Some dealers will bring the customer to the auction, although the dealer may have his or her buying card revoked by the auction if caught doing this. Other dealers will take a description of the vehicle as an open "buy order," then buy the particular type of vehicle when it goes through the auction. Many states have licensing requirements that make it illegal for some of the dealers to purchase a particular vehicle for a customer at auction. Dealers caught in such activities will not only lose auction privileges, but may also have their dealer license revoked.

Typical auction fees are paid by the customer, not the auction, and range from $150 to $350, depending on the cost of the car, relationship with the customer, etc. The dealer may be reluctant to admit this type of income as the activity is discouraged by the auction.

The best way to check for this type of income is to obtain a print out of the vehicles purchased from auctions the dealer does business with and spot check the listings for inclusion into income. Check for cars that stand out. For instance, if a dealer primarily sells domestic "sleds," a $20,000 Mercedes SL sports car purchased at auction would be out of character. There may be various legitimate reasons for such a purchase, such as a ready made sale, or needing a leading car to put in a package deal with less desirable cars currently in inventory.

Bird Dog Fees are a form of commission payment also known as finder or referral fees. These fees are generated by:

1. Serving as a broker between two dealers/wholesalers, etc.

2. Finding a retail buyer for another dealer.

These fees are often paid in the form of a check written directly to the individual or in cash. Many dealers will claim these fees as an expense, but very few dealers claim the income. One examination uncovered $32,000 in broker fees for sales between dealers, none of which was reported as income.

Rebate Income

Dealers may offer life and disability insurance to the buyers at the time of sale. The policies are generally purchased from unrelated insurance companies, with the dealer receiving a commission from the sale of the insurance product. There is very little self-insuring through related insurance companies in the industry, due to the complexity of meeting the definition of an insurance company, and complying with the multitude of regulations set up by state insurance commissioners.

Referral fees from an insurance agent or agency are typically paid to the individual rather than the business name. The commission may be in cash, bartered insurance coverage, trips, etc. Such income can be found by reviewing either the deal files of the year under exam, or current deal files. Look for a particular agent writing most of the coverage.

Credit life and disability insurance (CLI) is usually offered in conjunction with financing and provides that if the insured event happens (that is, the buyer dies or becomes disabled), the buyer's note will be paid off by the insurance company. The commissions may range from 30 to 50 percent. If offered, CLI should be a large source of income.

Although most states allow car dealers to sell CLI and earn commission income on each policy sold by the dealer, some states -- Michigan, as an example, -- specifically prohibit car dealers and their employees from receiving any portion of the insurance premium attributable to the retail sale of a motor vehicle. Therefore, in states such as Michigan, it is common practice to an automobile dealer to establish a "dealer-related" insurance agency with a family member of the owner as an officer or owner of the dealer-related agency. Michigan law is violated if it can be shown that the dealer controls or manages the insurance company.

Auto dealerships in Michigan and states with similar laws may not deduct under IRC section 162(a) the commissions paid to the Finance and Insurance manager for the sale of CLI. These expenses do not relate to the dealership business, but rather to the "dealer-related" insurance agency. Michigan law further prohibits the dealer-related insurance agency from reimbursing the dealership for the dealer's actual costs incurred in connection with the sale of CLI.

If you are unsure of the laws regulating the sale of insurance by auto dealers in your state, contact your state Attorney General's Office, Department of Motor Vehicles, Department of Commerce, Financial Institutions Bureau, Insurance Bureau, or related state agencies for information.

Financing rebates may take several forms. They may be a reserve account set aside by the finance company for resource paper or aggregate loan performance. As the loan portfolio ages, some of the reserve may be refunded to the dealer. Some smaller finance sources may throw some kickbacks to the dealer for sending the finance company business.

In Commissioner v. Hansen, 360 U.S. 446 (1959), the Supreme Court held that an amount retained as a finance company reserve was a sale of installment paper and the amount of the purchase price retained and recorded as a liability to each dealer, in the dealer reserve account, must be accrued as income to the dealer since the dealer has a fixed right to such sums.

To find if this income exists, look at the dealer agreement with the finance company, loan proceeds and recorded income. The dealership should be asked to provide account statements to determine the transactions in the reserve account. A listing of contracts financed, the amount financed and the withheld amount should also be reviewed. Review the title work or lien, checking for common finance sources. If the dealer records deposit sources, you may be able to spot check the deposit slips.

Some dealers sell a lot of "sleds," which often have had some body or paint work. Also some dealers specialize in insurance rebuilds. It has been a common practice for body shops to inflate the costs of repairs and rebate the difference to the owner in cash.

Warranty Contracts

Used car dealers sell two basic types of extended service contracts. The first type is between the customer and an unrelated underwriter. The dealer is merely an agent for the underwriter and keeps as profit the difference between the sales price of the contract and the "cost" paid to the underwriter.

The second type is a contract between the customer and the dealer. For this type, the dealer may buy insurance covering his or her risk or be "self-insured." If the dealer buys insurance, the income and expenses should be reported according to Rev. Proc. 92-97 1992-2 C.B. 510 and Rev. Proc. 92-98 1992-2 C.B. 512. If the dealer is "self-insured," the sales price of the contract should be reported as income in the year the contract is sold and expenses deducted under IRC section 461(h).

Internal warranties are more profitable. These warranty accounts need to be carefully examined for proper reporting of income and expenses. Income and expenses should be reported according to Rev. Procs. 92-97 1992-2 C.B. 510 and 92-98 1992-2 C.B. 512.

Consignments

A secondary source of sales for dealers may be consigned cars. These are vehicles that are not owned by the dealer, but are sold for a customer. Typically, the owner will permit the dealer to sell the car for a stated price. To the extent that the dealer can sell the car for more than the stated price, the excess is the dealer's profit or commission on the sale. Generally, the consignor is responsible for any incidental charges, such as cleaning or reconditioning the car for sale. Those charges are usually subtracted from the amount due the owner from the sale. The buyer makes payment to the dealer, who in turn, will remit the stated price to the consignor after payment of liens and deductions for incidental costs. The consignment of the auto is usually evidenced by a written contract between the owner and the dealer, although different states may have specific requirements that the dealer must meet. Dealers generally do not include consigned cars in inventory until the sale of the car actually occurs. At that time, it is purchased from the consignor, at the agreed price, and put into inventory. This is normally when the vehicle is assigned a stock number.

Dealer Financing

Dealers will commonly receive commissions on sales of various financial products. Some dealers will make arrangements with finance companies to provide financing for their customers. The finance company will frequently pay the dealer a commission or "finder's fee" based on the amount of the loan, or a set fee per loan.

Another example of income earned by car dealerships from financing companies is a rate spread. A dealership may have made arrangements with a finance company to write loans at a set interest rate, 8 percent, for example. When a car buyer purchases an auto from the dealership, the dealership may write the loan for a higher interest rate, 10 percent for example. The excess interest generated by the higher rate would be paid to the dealership by the finance company and would be includible income. The rate spread in this example would be 2 percent, the difference in the rate the bank makes the funds available and the eventual rate charged to the car dealer.

A dealer financing his or her own sales (Buy Here/Pay Here Lot) will generally collect on the notes in one of two ways. First, and most obviously, he or she will get monthly or weekly payments over the term of the note. The portion of the monthly or weekly payment reflecting interest will be additional income to the dealer. The principal portion of the payment will reduce the receivable, since the income has already been recognized at the time of sale.

A common alternative method of collection is to sell the note or a number of notes (bulk sale) to a third party at a discounted amount. The discounts are often significant, usually exceeding 20 percent of the principal, and in some cases approaching 50 percent. In addition, the dealer may continue to have secondary liability for the note (a recourse note). The discount is deducted at the time that the note is sold, since the dealer is not entitled to any more collections on the note, and the usual accounting entry on a $5,000 note sold for 20 percent discount would be:

	DR	CR
Cash	4,000	
Discount on Note	1,000	
Notes Receivable		5,000

A detailed discussion of the sales and discounting of notes receivable can be found in the Related Finance Company section.

A dealer self-financing a sale will customarily keep a financing file. Since the financing transaction is regulated by both the state and federal governments under various statutes, a paper trail of the transaction must be maintained by the dealer. A financing file will usually contain the following documents:

- Note.

- Security Agreement.

- Disclosure Notices required by law (if not contained in the Note or Security Agreement).

- Credit Application and Credit Report, if appropriate.

- Vehicle Title. (Some states send the title to the owner, and provide a notation of lien on the title.) In those states, the dealer will not have physical possession of the title).

SALES TAXES, REGISTRATION & LICENSING FEES

Sales taxes and registration/license fees are collected by the dealer and paid to the state. In most states, used car dealers are required to charge sales tax on all retail sales. Many communities have their own retail sales taxes which the dealers are also required to collect. In several states, autos with a lien will be charged an additional fee to register the lien. The lien fee is normally passed on to the customer. New license plates may or may not be required when the vehicle is sold, depending of state law. If plates are necessary, many states require the dealer to collect the fee from the buyer and submit the additional amount to the state. The dealer may also have income from sales to other dealers or wholesalers and from the sale of vehicles at wholesale or retail auctions. Sales to other dealers are not subject to sales tax in many states. Check state and local laws to determine whether sales taxes are applied to wholesale auto transactions. Some dealers include these fees in gross receipts and deduct the amounts paid to the state as an expense. Other dealers will not include these amounts in income or expenses.

NON-TAXABLE RECEIPTS

There are several forms of non-taxable receipts. Most used car dealers have lines of credit or other loans with local banks. Loans are frequently transferred into the checking account electronically. These loans may not all appear in the general ledgers. Owners will also frequently put their own money into the business when there is a cash shortage. These loans may appear in the general ledger or adjusting entries.

Many used car dealers receive checks from customers that are returned for insufficient funds. These checks are redeposited in the dealer's account and may be included in income a second time if the accountant is preparing the sales from the deposit slips. These checks may pose a problem in verifying income based on deposit analysis.

INCOME REPORTING

There are certain issues in dealer income recognition that agents should consider during an audit. These include:

1. Not recording a trade-in on a sale, then selling the trade-in for cash. One way to avoid reporting all sales is by cash sales in which a trade-in is sold directly to a third party. The dealer takes a car in as a trade from customer A. Customer A signs the title, but the dealer does not put the car in inventory or show it on the dealsheet as a trade-in. The dealer then sells the car to customer B for cash and signs the title over to the customer. The dealer keeps the cash and the title shows a direct sale from customer A to customer B. There is no indication that the dealer was ever involved in the trade.

    Indications that this may be occurring include unidentified cash deposits, reconditioning costs incurred about the same time, but not allocated to vehicles, substantial sales discounts or sales contracts that show a trade-in allowance with no corresponding stock number assignment. However, substantial discounts are frequently given by dealers to get rid of overage vehicles, where a cash (no financing) sale occurs or in similar situations.

2. Reporting net sales based on financing obtained, omitting cash received. Comparing the sales contracts with the financing files should disclose this problem. Also, the state sales tax can be used to determine the sales price, which would include any cash paid.

3. Not reporting the sale of all cars purchased. Comparing the purchase of vehicles acquired by trade and at auctions to a subsequent sale of that vehicle can provide information on accuracy of sales figures. Also, a review of claimed travel expenses can lead to information about auctions attended where possible purchases occurred or sales were made. However, dealers often attend auctions where they make no purchases or sales.

4. Purchasing packaged cars, allocating the full cost of the package to only some of the units; then selling one or more units off the books. A review of the purchase documents may provide evidence of the number of cars purchased. Furthermore, an analysis of the cost assigned to the inventoried cars acquired in the package should be made for reasonableness. However, it is common for the buyer to assign a different value to each car in the package than the seller assigned. The buyer is not privy to the seller's allocations, and generally bases his or her allocation on the relative value of each vehicle in the package to him or her.

   Purchases from other dealers are generally similar to purchases from auctions. However, there may be no written record of the transaction, and the transfer of title probably will be by a reassignment of title to the purchasing dealer. Frequently, the dealer may make a package purchase. This is a purchase of several cars for a lump sum. The purchasing dealer should record the cost of the cars based on the ACV of each car to the total purchase price. The ACV of cars sold in a package can vary greatly since it is common to put one or two cars that are difficult to sell in a package, with the expectation that the purchaser will want the other cars in the package enough to accept the entire package. As with cars purchased at auctions, the cost of the car will be increased by any reconditioning costs incurred in preparing the car for sale.

   As mentioned above, dealers purchase cars as part of a package deal that are "clunkers." The dealer may know this at the time of purchase, in which case a low market value will be placed on the inventory value of the vehicle. At other times, a dealer will not realize it bought a "clunker" until reconditioning has begun. At this point in time, the dealer has two likely options:

   — Sell the car from his or her lot, or

   — Sell the car at an auction.

3-9

Either way, the likely result will be a loss on the sale of the vehicle and no further transactions with the other dealer.

5. Another method dealers may use to avoid reporting all income is to purchase four cars from an other dealer or at auction. The purchase document will show four cars purchased. The dealer then books three cars into inventory and sells the fourth car without reporting the sale on his or her books. If such activities are suspected, check with the auction house as a third party source.

6. The independent used car dealer may take almost anything as a trade-in. Boats, trailers, snowmobiles, campers, etc. may be accepted as a trade-in. These traded items may or may not end up on the lot for sale. The owner of the dealership may be getting personal use of these items and sell them on the side as personal property instead of inventory.

    Vehicles taken in as trades may not be issued a separate stock number. It is a common industry practice for the new trade-in to be assigned a new stock number that is a subset of the original stock number. For instance, a car with stock number 122 is sold and a 1988 Plymouth is taken in as a trade; the Plymouth will be assigned stock number 122A.

7. In some parts of the country, used car dealers have been found to be members of bartering clubs. For example, in Wisconsin, the dealer would receive "points" from the bartering club based on the value of the car, which could be spent on services or goods such as mechanical or body work on cars purchased for resale. Such activities are frequently not included as income.

8. Many dealers engaged in "Buy Here/Pay Here" operations may repossess the same vehicle several times before it is ultimately sold. The dealer reports the gain on the first repossession, but not on the subsequent repossessions. See Repossessions below for more information on this topic. Treatment of "Buy Here/Pay Here" operations are included in Chapter 8, Related Finance Company.

STATE DEPARTMENTS OF TRANSPORTATION/MOTOR VEHICLES

Some state Departments of Transportation require all car dealers to maintain a record book of all used cars purchased and sold. The details of this requirement are discussed in the section on inventory valuation. Use of this log will not only help in determining inventory and cost of goods sold, but also in verifying all items are included in gross receipts.

In some states, such as Virginia, the number of dealer's plates is based on gross receipts. Some other states base the plates on the number of salesmen or units sold. Wisconsin and other states will allow the dealer to have any number of dealer plates, as long as the dealer pays the fees for them. If your state is one in which the dealer plates are dependent on gross receipts, the number of dealer plates can give the examiner an idea of the correctness of the amount on the return.

REPOSSESSED VEHICLES

Repossessions are common in the used car industry. When a repossession occurs, the industry practice is to bring the car back into inventory at the vehicle's ACV, determined by the N.A.D.A. blue book or other Department of Transportation approved valuation guide. Likewise, the defaulting buyer receives a credit against the balance due for the ACV of the car. Alternatively, the dealer may obtain bids from other dealers or simply sell the car at an auction. In those cases, the buyer is credited with the net sales price of the car. State law often controls what the dealer can do with a repossession, how the repossessed car should be valued, or what sales procedures must be used to sell a repossessed car. Accordingly, where the dealer has substantial repossessions, state law on repossessions should be reviewed. Repossession costs increase the basis of the car. These costs can include attorney's fees, repossessor fees, repair costs and retitle fees.

Small dealers may have better experience with repossessions than the larger dealers because they see it as a money maker, or they require a larger percentage of the purchase price as a down payment. A deficiency can arise when the ACV is less than the amount owed, just as a gain can arise when the ACV is greater than the amount owed. For example, a car repossessed has an ACV of $1,800. The amount owed the dealer at the time of the default on the loan is $3,000. A $1,200 deficiency exists. Using the same ACV of $1,800 and the amount owed to the dealer at the time of the default on the loan of $1,500, the repossession would result in a $300 gain.

The dealer will try to collect the deficiency from the defaulting buyer, although state law will dictate what collection procedures may be used. The dealer will also resell the car, either in a private sale or at public auction. If the sales price is less than the ACV credited to the borrower, the dealer may attempt to collect the difference from the buyer. Likewise, if the sales price exceeds the ACV credited to the buyer, the deficiency is reduced by the excess of sales price over ACV. If the repossessed car is sold with an overage (sales price exceeds the amount owed the dealer), the overage is repaid to the owner of the vehicle. Such requirements may vary from state to state and may be shown on the contract.

Many dealers will create a new stock number for the repossession, while others will reassign (restock) the old number.

When a sale of personal property is reported under a deferred payment plan, the gain on a subsequent repossession is equal to the Fair Market Value (FMV) less the seller's basis in the instrument obligation and less any repossession costs. The basis of a repossession is the FMV on the day of repossession. The basis of the obligation is figured on its full face value or its fair market value at the time of the original sale, whichever was used to figure the gain or loss at the time of sale. From this amount, subtract all payments of principal received on the obligation. If only part of the obligation is discharged by the repossession, figure the basis in that part.

The fair market value is the price at which a willing buyer would purchase a vehicle from a willing seller with neither party being under any constraints to complete the transaction. The FMV can be different than the Actual Cash Value which is based on adjusted wholesale values.

(NOTE: Dealers can not use the installment method for reporting the sale of inventory items. -- See Chapter 2, Accounting Methods.)

Issues

Are gross receipts properly reported on the return?

Whether or not any gain or loss is properly reflected on repossessed vehicles.

Audit Techniques

1. Pre-audit planning should include the following steps:

    a. Look into the owner's/shareholder's standard of living prior to starting the audit. This may indicate he or she is living beyond the means shown on the return.

    b. Analyze prior and subsequent return information as percentages of Gross Profit. Large changes in percentage of Gross Profit may indicate need   for examination of a particular issue.

    c. Run a cash transaction record (Form 8300) check to determine if large amounts of cash are being received and/or deposited. This should be done before starting the examination.

d. Perform quick Cash-T on shareholder/owner based on return information.

e. Check with your state's corporate charter division for a listing of all corporations the owners are involved in as officers or directors.

2. Visit the business location, checking for additional income sources such as a body shop or garage for mechanical work, or other on site businesses such as related finance companies.

3. As with all items under examination, reconcile the gross receipts shown on the return with the amount per books.

4. Scan General Ledger for unusual entries such as:

a. Debits to Sales

b. Credits to Expense Accounts

c. Cash Over/Under Accounts.

5. Carefully review internal controls, particularly for who receives cash, makes the deposits, and records income. This is an important part of the initial interview.

6. If the dealership has poor internal controls or if there are indications of significant gross receipts, the use of indirect methods are appropriate. This holds true for all types of business entities.

7. If records are poor, ask for all of the dealsheets for the year and total them up. The total should be the sales for the year shown on the return. If this technique is used for medium and large dealers, test this for a month's sales prior to taking the time necessary to do this for the entire year.

8. Trace a few vehicles through the dealers's accounting system as they impact inventory, cost of sales, expenses and sales. This should be done for each category or type of sales transactions.

a. Cash disbursements should be reviewed to determine which vehicles have been purchased, and then the vehicles traced to their ultimate sale. Any unexplained cash disbursements should be analyzed.

b. Furthermore, sales prices of the purchased cars should be compared to the ultimate sales price, particularly where there is an indication that the cars were part of a packaged deal, to determine whether the cost of the packaged cars is properly allocated among the vehicles purchased.

    c. If it is not practical to conduct the gross receipts, purchases, inventory, trade-in and repossession techniques simultaneously for a few vehicles, these accounts should be done in sequence instead of jumping to other areas of the examination.

9. Determine if the dealer engages in bartering, and if so, how actions are handled on the books for income reporting purposes. This should be determined during the initial interview.

10. Determine if sales taxes and registration/licensing fees are included in income. This should be determined during the initial interview.

11. Determine if the dealer has received any prizes from auctions or other dealers. This issue is best addressed during the initial interview.

12. A comparison of the financing file with the customer file is one way to verify the sales price and terms of the deal.

13. Determine whether the dealer is offering in-house financing and how these sales are recorded. There should be an accounts receivable set up to reflect the amount due on the car and the full amount should be shown as a sale.

14. If in-house financing is provided:

    a. Sample financing agreements for proper income reporting of the sale.

    b. Determine whether interest and other customer charges are properly included as income.

    c. For a detailed discussion of the treatment of related finance companies, refer to the Related Finance Company section of this ATG.

15. Determine if the dealer has an arrangement with insurance or finance companies to provide customer financing or credit life insurance for the dealer's customers.

    a. If so, how much of a commission or fee does the dealer receive from the insurance or finance company?

    b. Are the fees or commissions included in the dealer's income, and if so, where on the return are they included?

c. Scan the cash receipts journal or ledger for recurring receipts from insurance and finance companies.

d. Be aware of the proper timing for inclusion into income any amounts held as finance reserves.

16. Review statements for all checking, savings and other investment accounts for the period under examination, and for the period under audit. It may be necessary to obtain personal account information as well as the business accounts.

17. Compare sample of entries in used car log to dealsheets to assure all cars sold were included in gross receipts.

18. Review cash receipts journal for unusual and small recurring entries. Recurring entries may indicate the dealer is reporting income under the installment method or receiving commissions from insurance or finance companies. Such entries may also indicate the dealer is leasing vehicles.

19. Review State Sales Tax returns to see if what is being reported for sales tax is in line with what is on the income tax returns.

20. Ask to see any Forms 8300 filed -- these may provide leads to additional audits. This should be done as part of the package audit. See Chapter 7, Required Filing Checks, for details on Form 8300.

21. Scan deposit slips for recurring deposits from individuals that may be on an installment sale plan or commissions from insurance and finance companies. The receipt of large amounts of cash from one individual may indicate an attempt to circumvent the large cash transaction reporting requirements by leasing out vehicles and then selling at the end of the lease for a minimal amount.

22. Trace auto jacket and dealsheets to accounts receivable and sales. If there are a large number of sales, use a sample to check the accounts receivable and sales.

23. Sample dealsheets for other sources of income such as fees, warranty plans, finance charges, etc.

24. Sample dealsheets for items such as boats, camper trailers, recreational vehicles, and snowmobiles that may have been taken as a trade-in. Look for personal use and eventual sales of these items.

25. Review other documents in the car jacket and customer file for financing, warranty, agreements, service tickets, and other possible sources of income.

26. Obtain the number of title transfers from your state Department of Motor Vehicles to cross check records. This technique should be used when there is evidence of unreported income. In most states, this information should be easy to obtain.

27. Determine whether the dealership is selling notes receivable to a related finance company. See Chapter 8, Related Finance Company, for details on transactions between the dealer and the related finance company.

28. Inquire about any previous state and local examinations the dealer may have had in the past, including Department of Motor Vehicle examinations of used car records.

29. Obtain a listing of title transfers from the State Department of Transportation/Motor Vehicles for a selected period of time (week or month) which can be used to verify these sales were recorded. This should be used when records are incomplete or the examiner suspects unreported sales.

30. When there is a firm indication of unreported sales, consider issuing a summons for records not provided by the taxpayer. This should not only include bank records, but should also include invoices, purchase contracts, and other source documents from auto auctions.

31. Recognition of gain or loss from the repossession of property reported under a deferred payment method is measured by the difference between the Fair Market Value of the property on the date of repossession and the seller's obligation satisfied by receipt of the property.

    a. Secure all car jackets pertaining to that particular journal entry where repossession occurred. Also secure the original sales documents in order to determine if the basis of the obligation at the time of repossession is correct.

    b. Subsequent years sales of the vehicles should be inspected to determine if the Fair Market Value assigned to the repossessed vehicle was accurate. Any material differences should be adjusted.

    c. Test the correctness of the gain or loss reported on the sale.

32. The following formula can be used as a guide when testing the correctness of the gain or loss upon repossession.

```
Full Face Value of Obligation                 $
Less:  all payments of principal received     $_____
Basis in obligation                           $

Plus:  any repossession expenses              $_____
                                              $
Less: Fair Market Value                       $_____
Gain(Loss) on repossession                    $
                                              =========
```

If Fair Market Value is greater than basis plus expenses, there is a gain on the repossession. If the Fair Market Value is less than the basis in the obligation and repossession expenses, there is a loss on the repossession and a bad debt is incurred.

33. To save time in examining repossessions, consider the following short cut approach:

   a. Determine which vehicles are out on a finance contract at year end. Verify the proper tax accounting for the final sale of these vehicles during the year (straight accrual method). Adjust as necessary.

   b. For each vehicle above, verify that the taxpayer's original tax basis was used in the last sale during the year. Adjust as necessary.

   c. Instead of making detailed recomputations of each repossession, determine the net cash received (exclusive of interest) on each repossession transaction during the year.

   d. Steps a and b result in the proper gross profit on the final sale during the year. Step c reflects the net repossession gain or loss during the year on sales not outstanding at yearend.

34. Audit techniques for Cash and Accounts Receivable are discussed in depth in Chapter 5, Balance Sheet.

This page intentionally left blank.

Chapter 4

COST OF GOODS SOLD/INVENTORY

INTRODUCTION TO COST OF GOODS SOLD/INVENTORY

The accounts associated with the cost of goods sold (that is, inventory, purchases, costs of labor) constitute the largest deduction on a used car dealer's tax return. Shown below is a sample computation of the cost of goods sold from Form 1120, Schedule A or Form 1040, Schedule C:

1.	Inventory at beginning of year:	$ 190,100
2.	Purchases:	3,194,700
3.	Cost of Labor:	15,000
4.	Other Costs:	48,743
5.	Total:	3,448,543
6.	Inventory at end of year:	256,500
7.	Cost of Goods Sold and/or Operations:	$ 3,192,043

Most of the journal entries and adjusting entries to the cost of goods sold and related accounts will be examined through the inventory account. The examiner may encounter poor records for purchases and inventory valuation.

Purchases

The purchase figure reported on the return may frequently be a "plug" in order to balance the cost of goods sold computation. This makes it very difficult, if not impossible, to reconcile the account. Instead of accepting the "plug" figure, it may be necessary to reconstruct the purchases and inventory from dealer data. This means taking the dealer's invoices, vouchers, and other source data, and creating your own set of books for purchases.

If there is a purchase journal or similar documentation available, scan for unusual items. The unusual items may include personal items and capital expenditures, which will result in exam adjustments.

Auctions

Autos purchased at auction are purchased for a bid price. Most auctions use a combination purchase and sales document that will show the purchase price and any related auction fees. This becomes the base cost of the car. This cost will be increased by any reconditioning costs incurred by the dealer in preparing the car for sale.

Purchases from Other Dealers

Purchases from other dealers are generally similar to purchases from auctions. However, there may be no written record of the transaction, and the transfer of title probably will be by a reassignment of title to the purchasing dealer. Frequently, the dealer may make a package purchase. This is a purchase of several cars for a lump sum. The purchasing dealer should record the cost of the cars based on the Actual Cash Value (ACV) of each car to the total purchase price. The ACV of cars sold in a package can vary greatly since it is common to put one or two cars that are difficult to sell in a package, with the expectation that the purchaser will want the other cars enough to accept the entire package. As with cars purchased at auctions, the cost of the car will be increased by any reconditioning costs incurred in preparing the car for sale.

Cost of Labor

Labor costs involved in reconditioning and delivery of autos are required to be included in cost of goods sold. The costs attributable to vehicles in ending inventory should be included as part of the inventory value. Labor costs may be incorrectly included in "outside services" or other such accounts.

Other Costs

Other costs may include reconditioning, parts, delivery, detailing, outside services, repairs, and subcontracting. This is another area in which capital or personal items may be hidden.

Reconditioning Expenses

A dealer will generally have substantial reconditioning expenses. These are the costs that must be incurred to get the traded car ready for sale. The total dollars spent on reconditioning cars may be one of a dealer's largest expenses, depending on the condition of vehicles normally purchased. The cost of reconditioning each car should be added to the inventory cost of the car.

Remanufactured Cores

If your dealer is engaged in servicing vehicles for repairs and/or warranty work and even reconditioning, he or she may purchase remanufactured parts (for example, carburetor, alternator). Generally, the price of the remanufactured part includes a charge for the "core." This is an amount that will be refunded to the dealer once the old part is returned. If the dealer has any cores on hand at yearend, they should be inventoried. For example, a part may cost $ 100 divided into two costs: $70 for the cost of rebuilding the part and a $30 core charge. The $70 may be an inventoriable cost if part of reconditioning a vehicle, or a current expense for repairs or warranty work. The $30 is inventoriable separately with other parts until the core is returned for credit. Although it is improper, the dealer may expense the entire $100 when the part is purchased and include the $30 core charge as income only when the core is returned.

INVENTORY VALUATION

Inventory valuation is a complex issue for a used car dealer. A dealer generally buys used cars from new car dealers, other used car dealers, wholesalers, or at auctions. In addition, a dealer also acquires cars when he or she sells a car and takes a trade-in. The cost of the vehicles will be increased by the costs incurred to prepare the car for resale. However, the method of determining the initial cost of an inventoried car will vary, depending on the source of the purchase.

ACCOUNTING RECORDS

The industry custom is to maintain a file of cars in inventory by stock numbers. A stock number should be assigned as each car is purchased. A list of the stock numbers on hand is maintained. The stock number of the car will be recorded in the customer file at the time of sale. Other dispositions of the cars, for scrap, at auction, etc., will be noted by the dealer. Special issues arise for consigned cars, as discussed later. Many smaller dealers do not assign stock numbers to their inventory, since the amount of inventory on hand at any given time is small.

Most dealers turn inventory quickly, selling acquired cars to retail customers, other dealers, wholesalers, or at auctions. Cars are sold at auction if the car is not sold off the lot in a very short period of time (90 to 120 days). It is also common for dealers to use the periodic inventory method, whereby inventory is taken at the end of the year. This is particularly true where lower priced cars are involved. It is also an industry custom to use the lower of cost or market method of inventory valuation. This usually results in some adjustment at yearend being made to the inventory. This adjustment may increase or decrease the cost of goods sold, depending on the inventory level. For dealers using the periodic method of inventory and the lower of cost or market, the following entry will generally be made each yearend to record any write-down of the inventory to market. In this example, the reduction is assumed to be $2,500:

	DR	CR
Cost of sales	2,500	
Inventory		2,500

Dealers that maintain stock numbers and record the costs on the individual cars can also have a write-down of inventory to market if they are using the lower of cost or market method. While the reduction should be noted on each vehicle, one entry, similar to the one above, may be made in the accounting records.

TRADE-INS

Some of the most complex inventory issues arise in the valuation of trade-ins. These complexities arise because the amount allowed as the trade-in does not usually equal the ACV, which is the initial inventory cost to the dealer. The various factors make the determination of value very difficult.

Cost Basis of a Trade-in

The starting point for determining the cost of a car taken in trade is the Actual Cash Value (ACV). It is a common industry practice to determine the ACV by the following steps:

1. Refer to a valuation guideline. While the KelleyBlue Book and N.A.D.A. Used Car Guide are two ofthe more common valuation guidelines, any guide line approved by the Department of Transportation is acceptable, including Auction guidelines. However, these books serve only as the starting point, as a guideline for the value of the car. Even the valuation guidelines point out that adjustments must be made for the actual condition of the car, since the guideline assumes an average condition. Many dealers may not follow proper tax procedures through the use of a published guideline, instead basing their determination on the actual market conditions existing at that time in their location.

2. The dealer will then adjust the value to into account specific features of the car that add to or subtract from the guideline value. Some of these factors include:

- Actual wear and tear on the car,

- Mileage,

- Accessories,

- Any hidden damage such as frame damage,

- The cost of complying with Environmental Protection Agency (EPA) requirements,

- Whether the car has been in an accident.

The dealer will also consider another intangible factor, the market conditions. This is a factor to be critical of, because it deviates from valuations provided in the published guidelines. For example, a convertible offered as a trade in November may have less value than one offered as a trade in April or July, since the opportunity to quickly resell the convertible depends on the season. (Clearly it is harder to sell a convertible when snow is falling than it is on a warm spring or summer day). **There are three problems with this type of write-down:**

a. **The actual cash value of the convertible will not change dramatically between November and December.**

b. **The car can be sold in a warmer climate for what it is worth, or more, because of greater demand for convertibles in warmer climates.**

c. **Tax law will not allow a write down of a vehicle when the facts show it will be worth substantially more only 4 or 5 months later.**

d. Other conditions such as the overall market for the particular car being offered for sale, safety recalls, or changes in the automobile industry can all impact the value of a car.

e. See Thor Power Tool v. Commissioner, 439 U.S. 522 (1979) and Saul S. Pearl v. Commissioner, T.C. Memo. 1977-26 later under References in this chapter for more information on inventory write-down.

3. The value of the car is then adjusted for reconditioning costs and other expected expenditures that the dealer will have to make to get the car ready for resale. Some common expenditures include:

- Cleaning the car

- Mechanical repairs

- Body damage repairs

- Interior and upholstery repairs

- Safety inspection

- Required state inspection

- Emissions control inspection

- Painting

- Tires

- Finder's Fees.

This is not intended to be an exhaustive list, but rather illustrative of the types of work that the dealer may have to perform to get the car ready for sale. This reconditioning work may or may not be done directly by the dealer. In many cases, the work will be subcontracted out.

Trade-in Valuation

The valuation of a trade-in is an art, not a science. This outline of the valuation process may or may not be followed by a particular dealer. Many dealers, for example, rely more on experience and personal judgment than on a valuation guide. Others may rely solely on their professional judgment of the value of the car in that area at that time. However, every dealer values that car for the sole purpose of making a profit on both the car in inventory and the trade-in, when it is ultimately sold.

Dealers may undervalue their yearend inventory to overstate the cost of goods sold by using unacceptable methods of valuation. For example, one dealer, Tom, used personal knowledge and yearend auction prices for similar cars as the means of valuing inventory. His reason for using auction value was that this was the price he could get for his cars if forced to dump his inventory at auction and close the business. This was not the dealer's primary market. Another dealer, Joe, was found to be using loan values to determine inventory value. Joe stated he could get better loans from the bank by using the loan value of the cars as his inventory value.

While the industry may recognize the use of experience and personal judgment to value inventory, the Internal Revenue Service and the courts do not accept such methods of valuation. The courts have ruled that <u>Kelley Blue Book</u> or another officially recognized valuation guide is to be used for tax purposes. See Brooks-Massey Dodge, Inc. and Revenue Ruling 67-107, 1967-1 C.B. 115 under references in this section for more information concerning proper inventory valuation.

Once the ACV of the trade-in is determined, then the trade-in allowance that will appear on the sales contract must be negotiated with the buyer. These negotiations often result in an overallowance, for various reasons. As indicated earlier, the sales price is usually adjusted to take the overallowance into account. Properly determining the ACV of a trade-in is critical to the dealer's success since the profit on sale of both the inventory and traded vehicles will ultimately be determined by how accurate a value is placed on the trade-in.

A problem may arise when the trade-in has a loan still outstanding. Some transactions will be upside down, with the outstanding loan amount greater than the ACV of the car. In those cases, the dealer will give the buyer a trade-in allowance equal to the loan balance. The excess of the loan amount over the vehicle's ACV is an overallowance which, in the industry, is treated as a discount to the sales price. The dealer will pay off the outstanding loan balance.

Example 1

Customer #1 wants to buy a car with an asking price of $5,000 (and a dealer cost of $4,000) and offers a trade in with an ACV of $2,500. The dealer wants to make $500 on the transaction. However, the payoff on the original loan on the car is $3,100. Thus the vehicle is upside down by $600. The dealer may well give the buyer a $3,100 trade allowance (the dealer will pay off the loan) to make the sale. If this occurs, the dealer's gross profit will only be $400, computed as follows:

Cash Received	$ 1,900	($5,000 - $3,100)
ACV of Trade-in	2,500	
Total Received	$ 4,400	
Cost of Car	(4,000)	
Gross Profit	$ 400	

Thus, in this example, the dealer did not make his $500 gross profit, instead settling for only a $400 gross profit, due to the loan payoff on the trade-in. Another way to calculate this is as follows:

Asking Price	$ 5,000
Less:	
Trade Allowed $ 3,100	
Less: Payoff (3,100)	-0-
Net to Pay	$ 5,000
ACV on Trade	2,500
Total Value to the Dealer	$ 7,500
Less: Loan Payoff	(3,100)
Net Value to the Dealer	$ 4,400
Less: Inventory Cost	(4,000)
Gross Profit	$ 400

However, the cost of the car to the dealer should be the $2,500 (the ACV), and the $600 excess of the trade-in allowance over the actual ACV should be treated as a sales discount. The entry shown below for customer 1 is a proper accounting entry. The entry for customer 2 is the entry more commonly found in books and records for the example above.

	CUSTOMER 1		CUSTOMER 2	
	DR	CR	DR	CR
Cash	1,900		1,900	
Purchases	2,500		2,500	
Discount	600			
Sales		5,000		4,400

Another common occurrence is that a vehicle acquired as a trade-in will be sold and another trade-in will be acquired. It is a common industry practice for the new trade-in to be assigned a new stock number that is a subset of the original stock number. For example, a trade-in acquired in the sale of stock #100 will be assigned stock #100A. A trade-in acquired in a subsequent sale of stock #100A will be assigned stock #100B and so forth.

There are several ways to record the purchase of inventory items. A typical entry for a dealer using a double entry accounting system would be:

	DR	CR
Purchases	2,300	
Cash		2,300

Single entry systems may be used by the smaller dealers. Records may be a check register or ledger sheet showing the purchases of inventory and other expenses listed together.

Some dealers will use a perpetual inventory method, whereby the inventory account is updated with each sale and purchase. With this method, the dealer will know the value of his or her inventory at any given time during the year. Adjustments to the inventory account and cost of sales may be made throughout the year, or one adjustment may be made at the end of the year. A majority of the dealers will take a periodic inventory, usually at the end of the year, and adjust the purchase, inventory and cost of goods sold accounts at that time.

When the dealer uses the periodic inventory method, a physical inventory is taken at yearend. The dealer may write the inventory down at this time and make one entry to record the inventory value less the write down. In such instances, that will be the only entry at yearend to establish inventory at the lower of cost or market. The dealer should maintain a record of the write down taken on each vehicle in inventory.

Yearend write-downs on used vehicles are allowable when certain requirements are met. Revenue Ruling 67-107 allows a car dealer to value his or her used cars for inventory purposes at valuations comparable to those listed in an official used car guide adjusted to conform to the average wholesale price listed at that time. (See also Brooks-Massey Dodge, Inc., 60 T.C. 884 (1973).) Although this is a practice recommended by the industry and used by nearly all car dealers, there are some additional requirements.

Treas. Reg. section 1.446-1(a)(2) states in part that a method of accounting which reflects the consistent application of generally accepted accounting principles in a particular trade or business in accordance with accepted conditions or practices in that trade or business will ordinarily be regarded as clearly reflecting income. Treas. Reg. section 1.471-2(d) provides that the method must be applied with reasonable consistency to the entire inventory of the taxpayer's trade or business. There is a lack of consistency if more than one official valuation guide is used simultaneously.

IRC section 471 provides that inventories must conform as nearly as may be to the best accounting practice in the trade or business and must clearly reflect income. These regulations under IRC section 471 prescribe two instances where inventory may be written down below cost to market. The first instance allows a taxpayer to write down purchased goods to replacement cost (Treas. Reg. section 1.471-4(a)).

The second instance is contained in Treas. Reg. section 1.471-4(b) which states in part that inventory may be valued at lower than replacement cost with correctness determined by actual sales for a reasonable period before and after the date of inventory. Prices which vary materially from the actual market prices during this period will not be accepted as reflecting market. (See also Thor Power Tool Co. v. Commissioner, 439, U.S. 522 (1979) and Saul S. Pearl v. Commissioner, T.C. Memo 1977-262.)

Review the sales of vehicles that have been written down and not unusually large profits.

The independent used car dealers may not keep accurate inventory records. They take a physical count of the cars on hand at the end of the year and place a value on them. The total value is given to their accountant who prepares the returns based on the amount provided. It may be necessary to have the dealer go back and physically reconstruct the inventory value from other records. Inventory and purchase records may consist of a folder or pile of purchase receipts, index cards, or a three-ring binder containing the purchase information on each vehicle.

For book purposes, cars and trucks are accounted for on a specific identification method. For tax purposes, most taxpayers use either the lower of cost or market method or the cost method. LIFO is very seldom used by used car dealers, but you may come across it. The Service holds that a taxpayer may use an official used car guide such as the Kelley Blue Book in determining its LIFO cost of trade-in vehicles. The taxpayer must make the determination of value at the time of trade-in and no future write-downs are permitted.

With respect to the taxpayer's index computation method, the proper method for computing the index for used vehicles is:

1. To use the taxpayer's own cost (actual for vehicles purchased and blue book value as of the trade-in date for vehicles obtained in a trade-in); and

2. to use the taxpayer's own cost (as described in #1) for the same type vehicle in the ending inventory of the preceding year, or, if there was no such vehicle in the ending inventory of the preceding year, use the "reconstruction" techniques contained in Treas. Reg. section 1.472-8(e)(2)(iii) for items not in existence and

items not stocked in the prior year -- that is, the blue book value for the same type of vehicle at the beginning of the year.

As with any method, problems can and do arise which were not originally anticipated. Included among these are program cars with a much higher value than "book" and there is no requirement to increase trade-in value to equal "book" value. In addition, the costs of improvements are expensed and there is difficulty with objectively defining a comparable vehicle. If you find a LIFO inventory case, request assistance from a resource person.

Sometimes the independent used car dealers may drive cars from their lot for personal use such as commuting and vacations. Family members may also drive cars from the lot. These cars should be carried on the books as inventory available for customers; however, such cars are sometimes overlooked in determining the yearend inventory value.

Occasionally, vehicles will "disappear" from the inventory. Several reasons for this may exist. Older cars or cars in poor condition because of accidents or rust may have parts removed for repairs to other cars; then the body is scrapped. Such cars may be included in Cost of Goods Sold, but any income from the sale of the scrap metal etc., may not be reported in income. The same car may still be showing in the inventory, but is not on the dealer's lot. Another reason for disappearing inventory is that cars may be sold out of state, and thus, never show up on the Department of Motor Vehicle records for your state. Also the possibility exists that the dealer or his or her family is using one of these cars for personal use.

REPOSSESSIONS

Generally, used car dealers do not finance the sale of their automobiles. However, some dealers offer this service in an attempt to reach a segment of the market that cannot pay cash or secure other financing because of bad credit or no credit. The decision to offer financing is one that is made on a dealer-by-dealer basis and reflects the dealer's perception of the dealer's market.

When dealers provide a deferred payment plan (in-house financing), also called "Buy Here/Pay Here," there is the potential for repossession to occur. When a car is repossessed, the dealer must bring it back into inventory at its fair market value (FMV) and a gain or loss may result. The dealer should treat any gain or loss on repossession as ordinary income. For more detailed information on repossessions, see Chapter 3, Gross Receipts.

A demonstrator, which may include a vehicle driven for personal use, is a car that must be in current inventory and available for demonstration use while the employee is working. In Luhring Motor Co., Inc. v. Commissioner, 42 T.C. 732, 753 (1964), "The 42 vehicles in question [included in the demonstrator inventory account] never lost their inventory character and remained, even after several thousand miles of business use to which they were assigned by petitioner, automobiles properly includible in the stock in trade and held for sale to customers in the ordinary course of business" and were not depreciable. Further, in Rev. Rul. 75-538, 1975-2 C.B. 35, the Service ruled that a vehicle is not property used in the trade or business if it is merely used for demonstration purposes and thus a depreciation deduction under IRC section 167 is not allowable.

Generally, if a dealer is leasing vehicles, the leased vehicles are capital items subject to depreciation. The Service holds that "dual-purpose" property, that is, property offered for lease or sale, is properly includible in inventory. The taxpayer's main source of income is from sales not leasing. The Service considers whether the taxpayer's intent is to convert the use to leasing so that the items are no longer held for sale.

Revenue Ruling 55-540 contains guidelines to be used in determining the tax treatment of leases of equipment. If the lease agreement is, in substance, a conditional sales contract, the lessee is to be considered the owner of the equipment.

IRC section 263A and Treas. Reg. section 1.263A-1T detail the expenses to be included as part of the cost of the product. (Treas. Reg. sections 1.263A-1, 1.263A-2 and 1.263A-3 effective for tax years beginning after 1993.) These sections apply to real, tangible and intangible property acquired for resale. In most cases, IRC section 263A will not apply to an independent used car dealer because Gross Receipts fall under the $10,000,000 exemption.

ISSUES

Is the cost of goods sold properly reported?

Are all required costs included in the inventory? (Treas. Reg. section 1.471-2)

If IRC section 263A applies, have all required direct and indirect costs been applied to the inventory costs?

Are approved methods used to determine inventory values?

If Lower of Cost or Market is used, has the "Market" been properly reflected as defined in Treas. Reg. section 1.471-4(a)?

Is the write-down proper?

Are gains on repossessions properly reported?

GENERAL AUDIT TECHNIQUES

1. Not all dealers maintain accurate records, especially when it comes to ending inventory. Many dealers will take a count and give the amount to their accountant, who will enter the amount on the return. The dealer may not have a written copy of what he or she had in inventory at the end of the year. It is the dealer's responsibility to reconstruct the inventory valuation. Refer to the section on dealer licensing requirements to see what information your State Department of Motor Vehicles can provide concerning what the dealer has in inventory at the end of the year.

2. The initial document request for inventory information should include:

   a. The car jackets, which should include all purchase documents, sales documents, title transfers, odometer statements, and any other information pertaining to each car, such as receipts for all repairs and parts that apply to each car purchased during the year, or

   b. If the dealer does not maintain a jacket on each car, request all invoices relating to the purchase of each car, any additional costs such as repairs, and the odometer statements from the previous owner and the sale of the vehicles in inventory.

   c. Any stock records, inventory cards, etc., that the dealer used to establish his inventory valuations.

3. Review entries in the general ledger control accounts. Note and verify entries which originate from other than usual sources (general journal entries, debit and credit memos, etc.).

4. Review the cost of sales accounts and examine accounts that are material in accordance with standards set forth in the Expense Audit Guidelines (see SAIN Program 500,843:(1)).

5. Review the adjusting journal entries for proper treatment of cost of goods sold and inventory at yearend, as well as personal items purchased with business funds for proper reclassification of personal items. Be sure to understand the nature of the adjustment.

4-13

6. Sample dealsheets for trade-ins. Cross reference to the inventory and purchase accounts for proper inventory valuations.

7. If sales are recorded net of trade-ins, verify that the trade-ins are not included in cost of goods sold. The taxpayer should not be allowed to record sales at net. Net trades frequently occur in single entry accounting systems. The dealer will deduct the trade-in value from the sale price of the vehicle being purchased, resulting in a decrease in sales for the period. He or she may then include the trade-in value as a cost of goods sold when the trade-in is sold to another customer. Thus, the dealer gets to take the deduction of the trade-in twice, once when purchased and again when sold. To stop this from happening, require the taxpayer to record sales at gross, not at net.

8. If purchases are made from related taxpayers, review a representative number of these transactions to determine if the following are present:

   a. Excessive rebates and allowances, or

   b. Goods or services not received (this would be a good device to improperly withdraw funds and receive a resultant tax deduction).

9. Look for voided inventory transactions. Such transactions could be legitimate or they could be a wholesale trade off the books. Find out who the car was purchased from and ask them for third party verification on whether or not the vehicle was or was not returned.

10. Trace beginning inventory to final sale by looking at the sales jackets. Look for unreported and underreported income.

11. Reconstruct purchases and sales from the taxpayer's source documents. This may take some time, but you should feel comfortable that all sales data is there. Use this procedure when the taxpayer keeps very poor books.

12. Be wary of consignment sales. These vehicles may not have a stock number.

13. Look for personal vehicles included as purchases but not in ending inventory (jet ski's, boats, snowmobiles, etc.)

SPECIFIC AUDIT TECHNIQUES

1. Obtain any workpapers used in determining the yearend inventory valuation in addition to invoices and pricing guides.

2. For periodic inventory taxpayers, concentrate your efforts on yearend inventory valuations for all vehicles on hand, regardless of the source.

3. Question the taxpayer as to how yearend valuation was determined, and verify the method used conforms to prescribed methods found in Treas. Reg. section 1.471-2.

4. If Lower of Cost or Market is used, ascertain whether the method used to determine inventory values is at the acceptable industry market values. An accepted industry guide book may be used at arriving at this valuation. Two of the most common industry valuation guides are the <u>NADA Official Used Car Guide</u> and the <u>Kelley Blue Book</u>.

5. Assure the valuation guides are use properly and consistently. The dealer should be using same guide for valuing all inventory items, and not using a different guide for different cars because of a lower value shown in one guide for a certain car.

6. Review the jackets and invoices for repairs, parts, and labor to assure that all the costs incurred during the year of audit are included in inventory. These costs should be included in the year the work was accomplished or the parts purchased, not when these items were paid for by the dealer. Hiking or delivery costs should also be included as part of the inventory costs.

7. Compare a sample of the inventory values to the Blue Book or other valuation guide used by the dealer. In order to know which of the various models, trim level, and engine size to use in the Blue Book, you will need to look at the car's serial number. The Blue Book will tell you which positions in the serial number are used for the different makes to determine the model, trim level, and engine size.

8. Compare the subsequent sale of inventory items to the yearend inventory value. If the sales price is more than the inventory value, the write-down would appear to be improper. (Cost was lower than Market.)

9. Drive or walk by the business location to observe the level of business activity and inventory the business maintains. You may also find the dealer will have other items such as boats, recreational vehicles, motorcycles, campers, or other items on the lot. Follow-up to find out if these items were ever made available for resale.

10. If your state requires all wholesale and retail transactions to be reported, the Department of Motor Vehicles may be able to assist in establishing yearend inventory count.

11. Independent used car dealers may sell cars on consignment as well as from their own inventory. A quality initial interview should include questions concerning consignment sales. Verify proper inventory treatment of cars on consignment at yearend.

12. Drive by the owner(s') residence to make a preliminary determination of the standard of living and whether cars from the inventory are kept at home.

13. Scan the inventory cards for voids and out of sequence stock numbers. Question any missing or out of sequence stock numbers.

14. Check the cutoff date. Determine if yearend purchases have been recorded in the proper accounting period.

15. Review title transfer date and the date the sale was entered in the books for proper timing of sales and purchases.

16. Confirm the accuracy of the inventory count, especially regarding cars driven by the owner and family members. A quality initial interview should help uncover any irregularities.

17. Determine if the owners withdraw merchandise for personal use, such as parts or cars. If so, proper reductions should be made to purchases or cost of sales. Consider possible tax effect of such withdrawals to the recipients.

    a. Review the odometer statements, comparing the mileage when the dealer purchased the vehicle to the mileage when sold. Large differences may indicate unrecorded personal use.

    b. Review purchases for items remaining in the inventory for extended periods. Such items may indicate personal use.

18. Scan depreciation schedule to assure no inventory items are being depreciated.

    a. Ascertain whether demos are included in the inventory count. Demos are to be available for sale at all times, and as such are to be included in the inventory count; not treated as a capital item, subject to depreciation.

    b. Leased vehicles may or may not be treated as a capital asset subject to depreciation. Review a sample of lease documents. Determine whether these cars are actual leases, conditional sales contracts, or vehicles properly includible in inventory (for example, used by family members, employees, etc.).

19. Inventory turnover rates will vary from dealership to dealership. The National Independent Automobile Dealers Association does not have any statistics on average inventory turnover rates. These rates vary, depending on the dealer's location, market and types of cars sold.

20. Review auction acquisition dates to assure purchases are included in the proper accounting period.

21. If inventory and repair records are poor or nonexistent, suggest a percentage of the total repairs be included in inventory costs rather than attempting to reconstruct the repairs done to the cars in ending inventory.

22. Scan the purchases account in the disbursements journal, check register, etc., look for items unusual in amount and to payee or vendors not generally associated with products or services handled by the taxpayer.

23. Be aware there may be acquisitions from private individuals that are not recorded on the books.

24. Determine whether repossessed vehicles are carried at the proper values and any gains/losses are properly recorded.

    a. Secure all car jackets pertaining to that particular journal entry on which repossession occurred. Also secure the original sales documents to determine if the basis of the obligation at the time of repossession is correct.

    b. Subsequent year's sales of the vehicles should be inspected to determine if the Fair Market value assigned to the repossessed vehicle was accurate. Any material differences should be adjusted.

    c. If the amount of repossessions is small compared to the sales, do not waste examination time in this area.

REFERENCES

IRC section 471 requires the use of inventories whenever the production, purchase or sale of merchandise is an income-producing factor, with exception for certain farmers.

Treas. Reg. section 1.471-2 covers the acceptable methods of inventory valuation. The acceptable methods are Cost, Lower of Cost or Market, and LIFO. This regulation also states that costs incurred in preparing inventory items for sale are to be included in the inventory value.

Treas. Reg. section 1.471-4(b) states that where the taxpayer in the regular course of business has offered for sale merchandise at prices lower than the current price defined in Treas. Reg. section 1.471-4(a), the inventory may be allowed at such prices less direct cost of disposition, and the correctness of such prices will be determined by reference to the actual sales of the taxpayer for a reasonable period before and after the date of the inventory.

IRC section 263A and Temporary Treas. Reg. section 1.263A-1T detail the direct and indirect costs that are required to be included in the cost of the product. (Treas. Reg. sections 1.263A-1, 1.263A-2 and 1.263A-3 effective for tax years beginning after 1993.) The rules apply to real, tangible and intangible property acquired for resale. The regulations provide that IRC section 263A applies to inventories valued at cost, lower of cost or market (LCM), market, or LIFO. IRC section 263A does not apply to inventories valued at market under either the market method or the lower of cost or market method if the market valuation used by the taxpayer generally equals the property's fair market value. However, IRC section 263A does apply in determining the market value of any inventory for which market is determined with reference to replacement cost.

Thor Power Tool Co., 439 U.S. 522 (1979), The Supreme Court ruled an inventory write-down was not allowed where it was based on subjective estimates rather than objective evidence and the inventory items continue to be held for sale at their original prices.

Brooks-Massey Dodge, Inc., 60 T.C. 884 (1973), The valuation of a used car inventory at 80 percent of the National Auto Dealer Association (NADA) wholesale values was improper. Adjustments to 100 percent of NADA values were approved.

S&R Chevrolet Co., Inc., 93 F. Supp 950 (N. D. Iowa 1950), An automobile dealer could not value its closing inventory of used cars by deducting from the amount paid or allowed the customer as a trade-in, a reserve which represented the difference between the cost and estimated value of each car a year later.

Complete Finance Corporation, 80 T.C. 1062 (1983), The taxpayer corporations were writing down inventories of small auto parts to reflect an estimated decline in value due to "damaged, shopworn, or imperfect items," but did not offer the inventory for sale at a lower price to reflect the write down. The court held the write downs did not clearly reflect the corporation's income.

Saul S. Pearl, T.C. Memo 1977-262, The lower of cost or market value method used by a new and used machinery dealer failed to properly value inventory where the dealer had marked down machinery and consistently sold the items for prices greatly exceeding the assigned inventory values.

Revenue Ruling 67-107, 1967-1 C.B. 115, states that used cars taken in trade as part payment on the sales of cars by a car dealer may be valued, for inventory purposes, at valuations comparable to those listed in an official used car guide as the average wholesale prices for comparable cars.

SAMPLE WORKPAPERS

The following pages show one method of developing workpapers for the adjustments to inventory. These are based on a case in which the dealership marked down its inventory from cost to salvage value at a local auto auction using the owner's personal knowledge of the industry and end-of-year auction reports to arrive at the yearend inventory value. The taxpayer was unable to produce any verification of these values through records or auction reports for the years under audit.

Workpaper 1 is a sample document request for information concerning inventory records and valuation procedures. Some states require used car dealers to maintain a log of all used car transactions. If your state requires these logs, include them as part of your initial document request.

Workpapers 2a (Year 19AA), and 2b (Year 19BB) were used to determine the adjusted cost of the inventory items. This data was based on purchase documents and other information found in the jacket for each car.

Workpapers 3a and 3b further develop the adjustment. They show a comparison of the adjusted costs shown on workpapers 2a and 2b to the inventory value shown on the books, average wholesale prices, sales price as recorded by the taxpayer, and the amount of adjustment for each car in inventory. In these workpapers, the adjustments are the difference between the adjusted cost and the booked inventory value. Serial numbers shown are only the first 9 digits, which are used to determine the average wholesale prices in the valuation guides.

Workpaper 4 shows the summary of the adjustments to inventory as well as other adjustments affecting Cost of Goods Sold. Workpaper 4 compares the return to the audit results and shows the final adjustment to Cost of Goods Sold for the years under audit.

Workpapers 5 is a sample write-up of a Form 886A submitted to the taxpayer explaining inventory adjustments.

This page intentionally left blank.

```
                |    Department of the Treasury   |Request Number
Form 4564       |       Internal Revenue Service  |
Rev Jan 1984|        INFORMATION DOCUMENT REQUEST   |
TO: (Name of Taxpayer and Co. Div. or Branch)|Subject:
                                              |
                                              | _____
                                              |SAIN No.   |Submitted to:
                                              |           |
                                              | _____|_____
                                              |Dates of Previous Requests
                                              |
_____|
```

The following information is required to make an evaluation of your inventory valuation for the year under examination:

1 Jackets for the inventory items listed on the attached sheet, including all documents associated with each vehicle, if maintained.

2 Invoices for repairs and other costs associated with preparing the cars for sale for all cars in inventory at the end of 19XX.

3 Purchase documents for a sample of the cars in inventory at the end of 19XX.

4 Purchase documents for a sample of cars purchased in the months of October, November, and December 19XX.

5 State used car record book for 19XX.

6 Stock records, inventory cards, valuation guides, work sheets and all other documents used to determine yearend inventory valuation for 19XX.

```
        |Name and Title of Requestor              |Date
F       |                                         |
r       |_____|_____
o       |Office Location
m       |
        |_____
```

This page intentionally left blank.

NAME: DATE:

YEAR: 19AA   AGENT:

ISSUE: INVENTORY ON 12/31/AA

SERIAL NUMBER	YEAR	MODEL	COST	REPAIRS	ADJUSTED COST	PURCH FROM	PURCH DATE
JMIBF232	88	MAZDA	1000.00	200.00	1200.00	WHOLESALE DISTRIBUTOR	03/07/90
IG3HN373	86	OLDS	2500.00	2441.25	4941.25	WHOLESALE DISTRIBUTOR	05/02/90
JT4YR27V	84	TOYOTA VAN	1250.00	2341.80	3591.80	WHOLESALE DISTRIBUTOR	05/02/90
IG6AD478	82	CADILLAC	1750.00		1750.00	AUCTION	07/11/90
IB3B218C	83	OMNI	100.00		100.00	TRADE-IN	07/13/90
JT2AE82E	87	TOYOTA	2500.00	2198.66	4698.66	WHOLESALE DISTRIBUTOR	07/25/90
11602412	77	MERCEDES	2550.00	512.36	3062.36	DEALER	08/01/90
1MEBP923	86	COUGAR	2675.00		2675.00	AUCTION	08/08/90
IG5CT18B	84	JIMMY	2800.00	1566.39	4366.39	WHOLESALE DISTRIBUTOR	09/05/90
IG3GR47A	85	CUTLASS	2225.00		2225.00	AUCTION	09/26/90
1XMAC996	86	ENCORE	1000.00		1000.00	AUCTION	10/17/90
1GIBN69H	86	CAPRICE	2295.00	225.32	2520.32	AUCTION	10/17/90
IG3AR47A	84	CUTLASS	2485.00		2485.00	TRADE-IN	10/23/90
IGIAW359	83	CHEV WAGON	800.00		800.00	AUCTION	10/24/90
IGIAX68R	83	CITATION	700.00	0.00	700.00	AUCTION	10/24/90
IG3AJ11R	88	CUTLASS	1995.00	1228.36	3223.36	AUCTION	10/24/90
JFIAC34B	86	SUBARU	2250.00		2250.00	AUCTION	10/24/90
1MEBP88F	82	MERC WAGON	300.00		300.00	AUCTION	10/24/90
JNIHM15P	90	NISSAN	3895.00	2453.91	6348.91	WHOLESALE DISTRIBUTOR	10/31/90
JT3EL36M	90	TOYOTA	1155.00		1155.00	WHOLESALE DISTRIBUTOR	10/31/90
IB3BM18C	86	HORIZON	1685.00		1685.00	AUCTION	10/31/90
IL47JAJ1	80	CHEV IMPALA	605.00		605.00	TRADE-IN	11/09/90
P39J6H54	76	BUICK	485.00		485.00	TRADE-IN	12/05/90
1VWAA017	83	VOLKSWAGON	495.00		495.00	AUCTION	12/12/90
1GGAL578	84	CADILLAC	1635.00		1635.00	AUCTION	12/12/90
IG4A257Y	82	BUICK RIV	1095.00		1095.00	AUCTION	12/12/90
IGIJC146	90	CAVALIER	2545.00	40.00	2585.00	WHOLESALE DISTRIBUTOR	12/12/90
IB3BD49C	84	ARIES WAGON	1485.00		1485.00	TRADE-IN	12/13/90
IQ8769L5	79	CAMERO	985.00		985.00	TRADE-IN	12/20/90
1VWDC017	83	VW GTI	710.00		710.00	AUCTION	12/20/90
4H87A8ZI	78	BUICK	100.00		100.00	TRADE-IN	12/21/90

			COST	REPAIRS	ADJUSTED COST		
Total			48050.00	13208.05	61258.05		
Inventory 12/31			24775.00	========	24775.00		
Difference			23275.00		36483.05		

4-23

This page intentionally left blank.

19BB Adjusted Costs

NAME:		DATE:
YEAR:	19BB	AGENT:
ISSUE:	INVENTORY ON 12/31/BB	

SERIAL NUMBER	YEAR	MODEL	COST	REPAIRS	ADJUSTED COST	PURCH FROM	PURCH DATE
2BAFK41C	84	DODGE CARAVAN	2,500.00	575.00	3,075.00	WHOLESALE DISTRIBUTOR	03/13
1AMCAC55	83	CONCORD	200.00	300.00	500.00	AUCTION	05/08
IG2NEIU6	87	GRAND AM	2,400.00	1,285.00	3,685.00	AUCTION	05/08
TKR149J5	79	GMC TRUCK	625.00	275.36	900.36	AUCTION	05/23
1J735969	79	YAMAHA	425.00	0.00	425.00	WHOLESALE DISTRIBUTOR	05/29
1VEFBO17	82	VW	200.00	250.00	450.00	WHOLESALE DISTRIBUTOR	05/29
1AMCDC96	85	ENCORE	300.00	850.00	1,150.00	AUCTION	06/19
IGILV14W	89	CHEV BARRETTA	2,850.00	2,375.00	5,225.00	AUCTION	06/26
IG4JS21K	87	BUICK SKYLARK	2,100.00	100.00	2,200.00	AUCTION	07/17
1MEBP18C	81	MERC LYNX	325.00	0.00	325.00	AUCTION	08/21
JMGC2210	87	MAZDA	1,900.00	895.45	2,795.45	WHOLESALE DISTRIBUTOR	08/28
1MRPM36X	88	TOPAZ METRO	1,600.00	1,800.00	3,400.00	AUCTION	09/04
	73	MARLIN	450.00	299.54	749.54	WHOLESALE DISTRIBUTOR	09/19
2L69HAP1	80	PONTIAC	75.00	0.00	75.00	TRADE-IN	09/20
IMEBM604	88	COUGAR	3,475.00	1,800.00	5,275.00	WHOLESALE DISTRIBUTOR	10102
1FMCU14T	88	BRONCO II	4,395.00	2,300.32	6,695.32	WHOLESALE DISTRIBUTOR	10102
IGIFP87F	86	CAMERO	4,925.00	1,875.32	6,800.32	TRADE-IN	10/07
53820634	78	VW	250.00	74.92	324.92	WHOLESALE DISTRIBUTOR	10122
IG4AZ57Y	82	BUICK RIVERA	500.00	525.23	1,025.23	AUCTION	10/23
4L69SAH2	80	BUICK	100.00	125.23	225.23	TRADE-IN	10/29
IG2A587I	84	PONT FIREBIRD	900.00	1,894.68	2,794.68	AUCTION	10/30
IG4EZ57Y	85	BUICK RIVERA	1,325.00	1,050.68	2,375.68	WHOLESALE DISTRIBUTOR	10/30
JT2CAG4L	82	TOYOTA	475.00	100.42	575.42	WHOLESALE DISTRIBUTOR	11/13
IG6J651E	87	CADILLAC	2,550.00	279.63	2,829.63	WHOLESALE DISTRIBUTOR	11/13
1GG2FS87	85	PONT FIREBIRD	1,500.00	1,099.58	2,599.58	WHOLESALE DISTRIBUTOR	11/13
IGIAZ37H	84	MONTE CARLO	2,125.00	324.78	2,449.78	WHOLESALE DISTRIBUTOR	11/13
JHMAH732	86	HONDA CIVIC	1,560.00	764.55	2,324.55	WHOLESALE DISTRIBUTOR	11/13
IG4H35N7	81	BUICK WAGON DIESEL	450.00	250.36	700.36	TRADE-IN	11/18
IG4AV35Y	83	BUICK WAGON	845.00	504.99	1,349.99	AUCTION	11/27
IN6ND115	88	NISSAN TRUCK	1,025.00	124.98	1,149.98	WHOLESALE DISTRIBUTOR	11/27
JHMAK343	85	HONDA	1,450.00	1,149.92	2,599.92	WHOLESALE DISTRIBUTOR	11/27
JB3BG39D	87	COLT	1,950.00	1,069.23	3,019.23	WHOLESALE DISTRIBUTOR	11/27
JHMEC142	87	HONDA CRX	2,255.00	900.21	3,155.21	WHOLESALE DISTRIBUTOR	12/13
JTA16MCO	77	JEEP	650.00		650.00	TRADE-IN	12/13
1MEBP783	82	MERCURY WAGON	1,400.00		1,400.00	AUCTION	12/18
1FHPP989	89	FORD ESCORT WAGON	1,300.00	845.62	2,145.62	TRADE-IN	12/18
JHMAH732	86	HONDA	1,300.00	1,419.66	2,719.66	WHOLESALE DISTRIBUTOR	12/26

Total			52,655.00	27,485.66	80,140.66
Inventory 12/31			32,720.00	========	32,720.00
Difference			19,935.00		47,420.66

This page intentionally left blank.

NAME: DATE:

YEAR: 19AA   AGENT:

ISSUE: INVENTORY ON 12/31/AA

SERIAL NUMBER	YEAR	MODEL	RED BOOK VALUE $$	SALES PRICE	ADJUSTED COST	INV VALUE	ADJUSTMENT
JMIEF232	88	MAZDA	3,100.00	1,500.00	1,200.00	325.00	875.00
IG3HN373	86	OLDS	5,800.00	5,295.00	4,941.25	925.00	4,016.25
JT4YR27V	84	TOYOTA VAN	2,000.00	4,995.00	2,000.00	1,000.00	1,500.00
IG6AD478	82	CADILLAC	1,831.80	2,700.00	1,750.00	550.00	1,200.00
IB3B218C	83	OMNI	100.00	100.00	100.00	50.00	50.00
JT2AE82E	87	TOYOTA	3,875.00	4,895.00	3,875.00	950.00	2,925.00
11602412	77	MERCEDES	2,400.00	4,500.00	3,062.36	1,250.00	1,812.36
1MEBP923	86	COUGAR	4,675.00	3,995.00	2,675.00	1,425.00	1,250.00
IG5CT18B	84	JIMMY	2,629.32	5,995.00	4,366.39	2,350.00	2,016.39
IG3GR4@A	85	CUTLASS	4,600.00	2,800.00	2,225.00	750.00	1,475.00
1XMAC996	86	ENCORE	1,975.00	1,900.00	1,000.00	525.00	475.00
IGIBN69H	86	CAPRICE	5,300.00	3,010.00	2,520.32	800.00	1,720.32
IG3AR47A	84	CUTLASS	2,775.00	2,995.00	2,485.00	1,250.00	1,235.00
IGIAW359	83	CHEV WAGON	1,625.00	995.00	800.00	400.00	400.00
IGIAX68R	83	CITATION	1,075.00	2,295.00	700.00	200.00	500.00
IG3AJ11R	88	CUTLASS	6,225.00	5,495.00	3,223.36	1,325.00	1,898.36
JFIAC34B	86	SUBARU	2,650.00	2,400.00	2,250.00	1,325.00	925.00
1MEBP88F	82	MERC WAGON	290.00	600.00	300.00	175.00	125.00
JNIHM15P	90	NISSAN	5,364.27	10,000.00	6,348.91	1,850.00	4,498.91
JT3EL36M	90	TOYOTA	4,750.00	4,995.00	1,155.00	925.00	230.00
IB3BM18C	86	HORIZON	2,050.00	2,195.00	1,685.00	900.00	785.00
IL47JAJ1	80	CHEV IMPALA	75.00	695.00	605.00	250.00	355.00
P39J6H54	76	BUICK	25.00	525.00	485.00	75.00	410.00
1VWAA017	83	VOLKSWAGON	1,450.00	600.00	495.00	225.00	270.00
IG6AL578	84	CADILLAC	5,875.00	3,850.00	1,635.00	850.00	785.00
IG4A257Y	82	BUICK RIV	1,015.00	2,109.52	1,095.00	950.00	145.00
IGIJC146	90	CAVALIER	6,125.00	6,995.00	2,585.00	1,300.00	1,285.00
IB3BD49C	84	ARIES WAGON	1,275.00	1,600.00	1,485.00	825.00	660.00
IQ8769L5	79	CAMERO	450.00	1,150.00	985.00	625.00	360.00
1VWDC017	83	VW GTI	1,775.00	800.00	710.00	400.00	310.00
4H87A8ZI	78	BUICK	50.00	387.00	100.00	25.00	75.00
Total			83,205.39	92,366.52	58,842.59	24,775.00	34,067.59
Inventory 12/31			24,775.00	========	24,775.00		=========================
Difference			58,430.39		34,067.59		
			========		========		

$$ DECEMBER 19AA STATE OFFICIAL USED CAR GUIDE AVERAGE WHOLESALE PRICES

This page intentionally left blank.

NAME: DATE:

YEAR: 19BB   AGENT:

ISSUE: INVENTORY ON 12/31/BB

SERIAL NUMBER	YEAR	MODEL	RED BOOK VALUE ##	SALES PRICE	ADJUSTED COST	INV VALUE	ADJUSTMENT
2BAFK41C	84	DODGE CARAVAN	3,525.00	3,700.00	3075.00	1,250.00	1,825.00
1AMCAC55	83	CONCORD	370.00	600.00	500.00	160.00	340.00
IG2NEIU6	87	GRAND AM	4,050.00	4,400.00	3685.00	1,350.00	2,335.00
TKR149J5	79	GMC TRUCK	965.00		900.36	425.00	475.36
lj735969	79	YAMAHA	400.00	500.00	425.00	100.00	325.00
1VEFBO17	82	VW	435.00		450.00	125.00	325.00
1AMCDC96	85	ENCORE	875.00		1150.00	850.00	300.00
IGILV14W	89	CHEV BARRETTA	6,175.00	6,700.00	5225.00	2,650.00	2,575.00
IG4JS21K	87	BUICK SKYLARK	3,675.00	2,755.00	2200.00	600.00	1,600.00
1MEBP18C	81	MERC LYNX	450.00	425.00	325.00	200.00	125.00
JMGC2210	87	MAZDA	4,425.00	3,825.00	2795.45	1,125.00	1,670.45
1MRPM36X	88	TOPAZ METRO	4,675.00	4,000.00	3400.00	775.00	2,625.00
	73	MARLIN	670.00		749.54	225.00	524.54
2L69HAP1	80	PONTIAC	100.00	90.00	75.00	25.00	50.00
1MEBM604	88	COUGAR	5,700.00	5,800.00	5275.00	3,000.00	2,275.00
1FMCU14T	88	BRONCO II	4,605.32	8,300.00	6695.32	2,900.00	3,795.32
IGIFP87F	86	CAMERO	5,475.00	7,000.00	6800.32	4,100.00	2,700.32
53820634	78	VW	290.00	475.00	324.92	150.00	174.92
IG4AZ57Y	82	BUICK RIVERA	840.00	1,900.00	1025.23	600.00	425.23
4L69SAH2	80	BUICK	100.00	900.00	225.23	100.00	125.23
IG2A587I	84	PONT FIREBIRD	2,075.00	3,500.00	2794.68	750.00	2,044.68
IG4EZ57Y	85	BUICK RIVERA	4,300.00	3,000.00	2375.68	895.00	1,480.68
JT2CAG4L	82	TOYOTA	435.00	650.00	575.42	150.00	425.42
IG6J651E	87	CADILLAC	4,475.00	3,800.00	2829.63	990.00	1,839.63
1GG2FS87	85	PONT FIREBIRD	2,500.00	3,300.00	2599.58	725.00	1,874.58
IGIAZ37H	84	MONTE CARLO	2,325.00	3,250.00	2449.78	700.00	1,749.78
JHMAH732	86	HONDA CIVIC	2,800.00	3,400.00	2324.55	350.00	1,974.55
IG4H35N7	81	BUICK WAGON DIESEL	700.00		700.36	300.00	400.36
IG4AV35Y	83	BUICK WAGON	1,340.00	2,095.00	1349.99	900.00	449.99
IN6ND115	88	NISSAN TRUCK	4,000.00		1149.98	600.00	549.98
JHMAK343	85	HONDA	2,175.00	3,425.00	2599.92	800.00	1,799.92
JB3BG39D	87	COLT	3,450.00	3,845.00	3019.23	1,400.00	1,619.23
JHMEC142	87	HONDA CRX	4,150.00	4,250.00	3155.21	1,100.00	2,055.21
JTA16MCO	77	JEEP	650.00	800.00	650.00	250.00	400.00
1MEBP783	82	MERCURY WAGON	1,350.00		1400.00	800.00	600.00
1FHPP989	89	FORD ESCORT WAGON	4,250.00	2,800.00	2145.62	850.00	1,295.62
JHMAH732	86	HONDA	2,800.00	3,000.00	2719.66	450.00	2,269.66
Total			91,575.32	92,485.00	80,140.66	32,720.00	47,420.66
Inventory 12/31			32,720.00	=========	32,720.00	==================	
Difference			58,855.32		47,420.66		

DECEMBER 19BB STATE OFFICIAL USED CAR GUIDE AVERAGE WHOLESALE PRICES

This page intentionally left blank.

NAME: DATE:

YEARS   19AA/19BB   AGENT:

ISSUE: COST OF GOODS SOLD

===

	19AA	19BB
ACTUAL COST	48,050.00	52,655.00
REPAIRS NOT CAPITALIZED	13,208.05	27,485.66
INVENTORY AT COST 12/31	58,842.59	80,140.66
INVENTORY AT MARKET 12/31	83,205.39	91,575.32
DIFFERENCE COST/MARKET	(24,362.80)	(11,434.66)

	19AA		19BB	
	PER RETURN	PER AUDIT	PER RETURN	PER AUDIT
INVENTORY 01/01	19,225.00	19,225.00	24,775.00	58,842.59
PURCHASES	344,429.00	344,429.00	304,699.00	304,699.00
COST OF LABOR	46,521.00	46,521.00	13,825.00	13,825.00
MATERIAL/SUPPL	0.00	0.00	0.00	0.00
OTHER COSTS	0.00	0.00	0.00	0.00
	410,175.00	410,175.00	343,299.00	377,366.59
INVENTORY 12/31	24,775.00	58,842.59	32,720.00	80,140.66
COST OF GOODS SOLD	385,400.00	351,332.41	310,579.00	297,225.93
ADJUSTMENT:		34,069.39		13,353.07

This page intentionally left blank.

Form 886-A	EXPLANATION OF ITEMS	Schedule No., or Exhibit
Name of Taxpayer		Year/Period

The proposed adjustments represent an increase in the value of this taxpayer's Used Car Inventory.

	12-31-___	12-31-___
Increase ending inventory:		
Increase beginning inventory:	_____	_____
Net proposed adjustment:		
	=========	=========

ISSUE:

Does this taxpayer's value of the used vehicle inventory properly reflect "Market" as defined in Treas. Reg. section 1.471-4(a) as the "current bid price prevailing at the date of inventory for the particular merchandise in the volume in which is usually purchased by the taxpayer?"

FACTS:

The taxpayer, _____, Inc. is a corporation organized and existing in the state of _____, with its principal office located in xxxxxxx, xx. During the years in issue, the taxpayer filed its federal corporate income tax returns on a calendar year basis with the Internal Revenue Service Center, reporting its income primarily under the accrual method of accounting.

The corporation has been in existence since 19--, and had an opening inventory of $___,___ in 19--. The corporation operates primarily as a retail used car dealership, but does sell some used cars on the wholesale market. The wholesale market comprises approximately ten (10) per cent of its sales.

At the end of each calendar year of operations, including the years ended December 31, 19-- and December 31, 19--, the taxpayer takes a physical inventory of all used vehicles on hand and marks the inventory value of each vehicle at what they estimate to be the average wholesale value. They do not use the National Automobile Dealers Association (NADA) average wholesale value. They do not use actual fair market value based on current sales of similar automobiles, or the most recent sales as a guide in establishing fair market value. They also do not use the most recent purchases as a guide in establishing market values based on most recent purchases. The returns show the inventory as being reported for tax purposes at cost.

Department of the Treasury - Internal Revenue Service Form 886-A

Form 886-A	EXPLANATION OF ITEMS	Schedule No., or Exhibit
Name of Taxpayer		Year/Period

The taxpayer appraises the inventory as an estimate of what he thinks he could sell that inventory at with only his experience to rely on, if the inventory had to be sold as a bulk sale referencing some auction values.

The closing inventory thus determined becomes the opening inventory for all of the used vehicles carried into the succeeding year. The used vehicle inventory values determined are used to compute the taxpayer's gross profit or loss from operations.

The taxpayer also takes trade-in on the sale of used vehicles and uses NADA as a guide to acquire the used cars taken in on trade.

During the years in issue, the taxpayer's valuation of its ending inventory was substantially lower than NADA valuations and the subsequent actual sale price of the used vehicles. The valuation was also substantially lower than most recent purchases.

The NADA average wholesale values used to compute the value of the taxpayer's ending inventory in 19-- and 19-- were taken from the December 19-- and 19-- issues of the Official **(STATE)** Automobile Valuation Guide. This guide is published eight times a year in collaboration with the (State) Automobile and Truck Dealers Association, and is an edition of Red Book. The guide sets out the average wholesale price for each make and model based on a thorough study of the used car market and does not apply to fleet, police or taxi cab sales.

The Government, in its review of this taxpayer's inventory values contends that the taxpayer's valuation technique is improper as it does not reflect the full market value of the used car inventory. Consequently this affects the yearend computation of profits or losses, thus the taxpayer's annual income in not clearly reflected. The NADA values, as computed, do accurately reflect true market value and the taxpayer's technique has not been established as a method sanctioned or widely used by members of the automobile industry.

LAW AND ARGUMENTS:

IRC section 471 gives the Government broad discretion in determining matters concerning accounting methods and the Government's discretion expressly extends to the proper use of inventories. *Photo-Sonics, Inc.*, 42 T.C. 926 (1964); *Dearborn Gage Co.*, 48 T.C. 190 (1967). Under the provisions of IRC section 471, the Government is delegated authority to decide which inventory accounting method is most suited to the taxpayer's business. The section additionally provides that in making this determination, the Government must be guided by two considerations:

Department of the Treasury - Internal Revenue Service Form 886-A

Form 886-A	EXPLANATION OF ITEMS	Schedule No., or Exhibit
Name of Taxpayer		Year/Period

    a. the best accounting practice in the taxpayer's trade or business, and

    b. the most accurate method of reflecting income.

The Government believes there is ample evidence in the record to raise questions about the effect of the taxpayer's valuation on the clear and accurate disclosure of its annual income. The increase in the taxpayer's taxable income attributable to the Government's change in the inventory indicates that the taxpayer, an accrual basis taxpayer, was unduly deferring a sizeable amount of income which should have been recognized in these years. Even stronger evidence of the imperfection inherent in the taxpayer's accounting system is the wide divergence between the value attributed by the taxpayer to its inventory and the NADA wholesale value of the inventory or the actual cash receipts realized from the sale of the same inventory. Moreover, the Government's choice of valuation in fact does clearly reflect income. Our findings of fact disclose that the computation of NADA wholesale values takes into account the wear and obsolescence of an automobile of a particular make, model and year in average condition. The record also indicates that, in the whole, the taxpayer's used car inventory during the years in issue was in average condition. Finally, the Government's position with regard to proper valuation of used car inventory has been on record for a reasonable length of time (see Revenue Ruling 67-107, 1967-1 C. B. 115), and the taxpayer is deemed to have known the Government's view.

The taxpayer states that he purchases 30 percent to 50 percent of his used vehicle inventory at automotive auctions at various locations throughout the central states. Since this is the market in which the taxpayer purchases a substantial amount of its inventory, it seems most appropriate to value the ending inventory by values on this same market. The taxpayer states he is using lower of cost or market rather than cost as shown on the returns.

The taxpayer does not use the NADA guide as the sole guide in the determination of value as vehicles are taken into inventory. The NADA guide is consulted, but the value is further adjusted by the condition of the individual vehicle, demand for the vehicle in the resale market and the estimated time to sell it wholesale or retail. This value approximates the cost to purchase a similar vehicle at automotive auctions held in the geographical area where the taxpayer normally purchases vehicles.

Form 886-A	EXPLANATION OF ITEMS	Schedule No., or Exhibit
Name of Taxpayer		Year/Period

The Government contends that the taxpayer's values of used car inventory for 1990 and 1991 do not clearly reflect income, nor is it a generally accepted practice to account for used vehicle inventory. The industry accepts and fully utilizes the NADA values. As such, the following adjustments to increase the taxpayer's ending used vehicle inventory are proposed.

See Workpapers 2a through 3b for calculations for the adjustments to inventory for 19-- and 19--. The net adjustments to inventory/cost of goods sold are calculated as follows:

	12-31-	12-31-
Increase ending inventory:		
Increase beginning inventory:	_____	_____
Net proposed adjustment:	========	========

Department of the Treasury - Internal Revenue Service   Form 886-A

Chapter 5

BALANCE SHEET

INTRODUCTION TO BALANCE SHEET

In some parts of the country the majority of the independent car dealers will not have a balance sheet with the return, as they will be sole proprietorships. The corporations and partnerships will usually have a balance sheet showing cash balance, inventory, fixed assets, other assets, short and long term liabilities, capital stock, and retained earnings. Dealers not using a hybrid accounting method should have accounts payable showing of the balance sheet. Accounts receivable may not be a factor if the dealer required all payments in full upon delivery of the vehicle to the customer.

Examination of the balance sheet for a used car dealer will not be as extensive as for a new car dealer. However, the balance sheet can reveal certain activities that may require examination. This section will focus only on those areas which may provide information leading to such adjustments as unreported income and personal use of assets.

CASH

Unlike the new car dealers, the independent used car dealers tend to have poor internal controls. The entire amount of checks and cash may not be deposited in the business accounts. Some dealers will provide financing or allow installment payments; however, the majority require payment in full upon delivery of the vehicle.

The independent used car dealer, as a rule, has only one or two bank accounts for the business. A checking account is the standard account for all used car dealers. Some may also have a business savings account, but this is extremely rare. Most dealers will have a line of credit or other loan arrangement with a financial institution and deposits will be made into the checking account as needed. Loans from the shareholder(s)/owner(s) are also frequently found in the used car business as a source of ready cash.

Issues

Is all income reported?

Has Form 8300 been filed as required?

Audit Techniques

1. For a detailed discussion of the filing requirements for Form 8300, see Chapter 7.

2. Reconcile bank statements to the books and the books to the return.

3. Review deposits slips for recurring payments from individuals. Be aware that many dealers only list the amounts of the checks on the deposit slips; therefore, it may be difficult to check for recurring payments using the deposit slips.

4. Perform indirect methods such as bank deposit analysis as necessary.

   a. One complication you may find is that many dealers will not include such collected items as sales tax and registration fees in gross receipts, but these duties will be deposited in the business checking account prior to payment to the state. These amounts must be taken into consideration when applying indirect methods.

   b. Another complication in performing indirect methods such as bank deposit analysis is that most dealers will have a line of credit with the local bank. Money from the credit line is frequently deposited in the business account to cover the purchase of inventory and to cover operating expenses. These loans must be considered when applying indirect methods.

   c. The independent used car dealer should be on the accrual method of accounting, however unless the dealer is providing financing or allowing installment payments to be made, the cash account will be a reasonable measure of the sales activity.

ACCOUNTS RECEIVABLE

While the new car dealers have very detailed receivables and separate schedules for each type, the independent used car dealer may have no detailed receivable information. Many used car dealer returns show no accounts receivable. They will not accept any terms other than cash on delivery of the vehicle. Others may allow selected buyers to pay a portion of the purchase on delivery and accept payments for the rest. The full amount may or may not be shown in gross receipts when the sale is made. Most frequently, the sales are recorded as the payments are received. The balance due may be kept in a separate book, index cards, or recorded on the dealsheets. IRC section 453 does not permit the deferral of income from an installation sale for a dealer that regularly sells or otherwise disposes of personal property.

The absence of accounts receivable or an unusually low amount may indicate that the dealer has discounted its receivables. See Chapter 8, Related Finance Companies, for information concerning discounting of accounts receivable.

Issues

Are all sales reported?

Are all sales reported in the proper tax year?

Audit Techniques

1. Sample deal sheets, checking for terms of the sale.

2. Review sales recorded in the opening days of the next tax year to determine whether the sales are includible in the year under examination.

3. Determine whether the full amount of the sales involving payment plans were recorded as income at the time of the sale.

Inventory

For a detailed discussion of inventory audit issues and techniques, refer to Chapter 4, Cost of Goods Sold.

Loans to Shareholders

Most of the corporate used car dealers are closely-held. You may often find that the closely-held corporations will have loans to shareholders.

There are two major items to be considered if loans to shareholders are found on the books. First, consider if the "loans" are bona fide loans. Often funds are withdrawn by the shareholder and treated as a loan to avoid taxes on the distribution. Care should be taken during examination to determine if a loan actually exists. If not, the withdrawals should be treated as constructive dividends provided the corporation has current or retained earnings.

Second, if a loan exists on the books, check for imputed interest. Determine if the loan is non-interest-bearing or at below-market rates. Since the Tax Reform Act of 1986 has phased out the deduction for personal interest expense, the income related to the loan cannot be offset dollar for dollar. Therefore, there will be additional income to the corporation, dividend income to the shareholder, but no deduction to the shareholder.

Issues

Is Interest Income being reported?

Are the transactions actually Constructive Dividends?

Audit Techniques

Refer to the INTERNAL REVENUE MANUAL and other training materials for specific audit procedures. Courts have considered various factors when deciding whether withdrawals are constructive dividends or loans. The absence of one or all of these factors may indicate the loan was made at less than in an arm's-length transaction and may be construed to be a constructive dividend and/or interest income.

Loans Versus Constructive Distributions

The following is a list of the factors the courts take into consideration when deciding whether withdrawals are constructive dividends or loans. No one factor alone is determinative but should be considered in total.

1. The extent the shareholder controls the corporation.

2. The corporation's history of paying dividends.

3. The existence of earnings and profits. It should be noted that the nonexistence of earnings or retained earnings is determinative of whether withdrawals are dividends.

4. The magnitude of the advances and whether a ceiling existed to limit the amount the corporation advanced.

    1) How the parties record the advances/withdrawals on the books and records.

2) Whether the parties executed notes.

   a) Are there written notes, maturity dates, interest charged? If interest was charged, was it at the market rate.

   b) Was security/collateral provided for the advances.

3) Was there a fixed schedule of repayment?

4) Evidence of the shareholder's intent to repay the loan.

5) Are there regular payments made toward reducing the loan balance?

6) Was interest paid or accrued?

7) The shareholder's position to repay the loan/advances.

8) Were the withdrawals/payments made in proportion to his or her stock holdings?

The 12 factors listed above are also applicable in determining whether advances from the shareholder should be treated as loans or contributions to capital.

References

IRC section 7872 covers the treatment of loans withbelow-market interest rates.

FIXED ASSETS

Ownership of fixed assets by the independent used car dealers is very similar to that of the new car dealerships. The shareholder/owner of the business owns the real estate and rents to the dealership. The business shows a rental expense and the owner shows income on Schedule E. See the Chapter 6, section on Rent Expense for a discussion of treatment of this issue by sole proprietorships. Any equipment, furniture, and fixtures are generally owned by the dealership.

Issues

Is the proper basis being used?

Is depreciation being properly determined?

Are personal assets included?

Audit Techniques

1. Reconcile the schedule of assets and accumulated depreciation to the tax return. If reconciling individual assets to the return is especially difficult, have the taxpayer reconcile his or her workpapers to the return.

2. Request invoices for large items for the years that have never been examined.

3. Physically inspect the assets to assure they are being used as business assets.

   a. Due to poor internal controls, the taxpayer may have difficulty locating some of the assets.

   b. Be constantly aware that in closely held businesses, the owner can purchase personal assets and deduct them through the books.

   c. An inspection of the assets on a surprise basis could indicate that some assets are located at the owner's residence.

LOANS FROM SHAREHOLDERS

Frequently, auto dealers will disguise capital stock as Loans from Shareholder(s). Special attention should be given to these loans if a company appears to be thinly capitalized. See IRC section 385. See Loans v. Constructive Distributions section for the 12 points to be used when determining whether advances from the shareholder are loans or contributions to capital.

Issues

Is interest expense properly computed and accrued?

Is the business adequately capitalized (thin capitalization)?

Audit Techniques

Analyze transactions involving loans from the shareholders to assure they are not designed to give the corporation a tax advantage. For example, the shareholder(s) may not want to have all their contributions classified as capital stock; therefore, they would classify a portion of this capital contribution as a Loan from

Shareholder(s). In this situation, the shareholder(s) would receive a return on capital in the form of interest income, and the corporation would deduct this portion as interest expense. See the Internal Revenue Manual and other training materials for specific audit procedures.

References

IRC section 385 deals with the treatment of certain interests in corporations as stock or indebtedness.

IRC section 7872 covers the treatment of loans with below-market interest rates.

SHORT TERM LIABILITIES

This account will generally consist of amounts due the bank for purchase of inventory items (flooring costs) which are due within one year. Dealers receive statements from the financial institution which provides the loans. Other liabilities such as payroll taxes, sales taxes, pensions, and reserves may also be classified as short term liabilities. Customer deposits may also show up as a short term liability.

Issue

Is interest expense properly computed and reported?

Audit Techniques

1. Ask the taxpayer to provide a reconciliation of the account. If the taxpayer does not provide it, you can determine the cut off date the bank used. Add   and delete vehicles that were purchased or sold during the period.

    a. Review the obligation arising from other than cash advances.

    b. Make a test computation of related expenses such as interest, payroll, and sales taxes, and trace them to the expense account.

OTHER CURRENT LIABILITIES

Generally, this account will include various accrued liabilities such as payroll taxes, sales tax, pension, and reserves. It is similar to the accounts payable and short term liabilities accounts. Dealers may arbitrarily classify amounts in any of these accounts.

Customer deposits may pose an income issue when they are associated with leasing. They may in fact be a disguised advance payment. It is common for customers to make an up-front payment called a "capital cost reduction" to lower their monthly lease rate. The Supreme Court's decision in Indianapolis Power & Light, 493 U.S. 203 (1990), gives a good insight to the difference between a deposit used as security collateral and an advance payment.

Issues

Are reserves for contingent liabilities included in the account?

Are expenses properly accrued?

Are customer deposits properly included in income?

Audit Techniques

1. Review reserve and allowance accounts to determine if they are for contingent liabilities, which are not deductible.

2. Review the customer deposit account to be assured that the deposits are included in gross income either when the sale is completed or if a "capital cost reduction" payment is made. Verify that any refunds of customer deposits are not expensed unless they were previously reported in gross receipts.

3. Review the accounts for unusual items that may indicate other business activities or personal items such as boat insurance paid for by the car dealership.

4. Trace unusual items to the related expense account.

DEFERRED INCOME ACCOUNTS

During examination you may encounter deferred income accounts contained in the balance sheet. Usually these accounts will be associated with the dealer's accounts receivable. They may have been netted against the receivables for presentation purposes.

Generally when a sale is financed by the dealer, he or she will pick up the entire sale at the time it is made (assuming he or she is using the correct accounting method). However, when the entries are made to record the retail sale of, for example, a $7,000 auto; down payment, the accounts receivable, and the related deferred income, they may generally be made similar to:

	DR	CR
Cash	1,000	
Accounts Receivable	9,000	
Sales		7,000
Deferred Interest Income		1,500
Deferred Contract Charges		1,500

The "contract charges" are usually separate charges for things such as procurement fees, processing fees, charges for investigation, appraisal and identification, etc. These fees are generally financed into the principal amount of the contract, and the customer is liable for them in total, with no discounting applicable for early pay-off. Interest on the contract is computed on the contract charges and unpaid selling price.

Example 1

An accrual basis auto dealer finances autos it sells. It includes the following three separately stated items in the purchase price:

1. Selling price of the auto,

2. Interest to be earned on the unpaid principal, which includes the selling price of the vehicle and the related contract charges, and

3. Contract fees associated with the sale, which vary greatly with each sale.

The financing notes, with interest rates of 29 percent or more, are subsequently assigned to a cash basis finance company. The finance company pays the auto dealer the unpaid balance on the selling price, and obtains rights to all unpaid interest and contract fees. The car dealer and finance company are related parties.

The finance company reports the contract fees as income at the time of payment, as if the contract fees are analogous to interest income. Treas. Reg. section 1.451-1 reaffirms that, under a proper accrual method of accounting, income is includible in gross income when all the events have occurred which fix the right to receive such income and the amount thereof can be determined with reasonable accuracy. Thus, the dealer must include the contract fees in income at the time of sale. If the auto dealer or finance company argue that these fees are actually interest, then the taxpayers breaks the truth in lending laws by charging interest far in excess of the rates disclosed in the contracts. Please contact your District MSSP Coordinator or the Motor Vehicle ISP for further assistance with this issue.

Issues

Are the deferred contract charges taxable income to the used car dealer in the year the sale is consummated?

If so, would the assignment of this income be considered a deemed distribution to the common shareholders, taxable to them as dividends?

Does the assignment of this note, at a discount to a related finance company, represent an arm's length transaction at fair market value?

Conclusion

The conclusion to be reached by the analysis of the facts cited above is that the deferred contract charges are not unstated contract interest, and therefore, are not amortizable over the contract lives. In addition, if the taxpayer contends that these fees are interest, then he is in violation of the truth in lending laws by charging better than 100 percent interest when the contract disclosure shows a much lower rate of interest.

The proper result should be to include the charges in the amount realized under IRC section 1001 per Rev. Rul. 79-292 1979-2 C.B. 287, for transactions consummated prior to April 4, 1994, and Treas. Reg. section 1.1001-1(g) for transactions consummated after April 4, 1994.

RETAINED EARNINGS

Retained earnings will be examined through Schedules M-1 and M-2 on the tax return. Schedule M-1 reconciles book income with return income. Schedule M-2 provides an analysis of retained earnings per books. Any dividend distributions and/or stock redemptions and retirement of treasury stock are reflected on M-2 as a reduction of retained earnings.

An examination regarding the applicability of the accumulated earnings tax (AET) should be considered. For an independent used car dealership doing business as a subchapter C corporation, the AET is a potentially significant issue. If a dealership is financially successful, it may decide to retain earnings at the corporate level, after paying the corporate tax, as a mean of avoiding individual income tax as to its stock at the shareholder level.

The M-1 adjustments are the differences between book income for financial purposes and taxable income for Federal tax purposes. Most of the adjustments are shown as adjusting journal entries on the accountant's workpapers. These adjustments include:

1. Federal Tax Liability

2. Officer's Life Insurance Premiums

3. ACRS over book depreciation

4. Penalties

5. 20 percent of the business meals and entertainment (Note: for tax years beginning after December 31, 1993, the amount allowable as a deduction for meal and entertainment expenses is limited to 50 percent of such expenses.

6. Restoring a portion of the reserves for bad debts, and repossessions.

7. Installment sales and income reported using the installment sales method in prior year. Installment sales do not include dealer dispositions, and inventories of personal property.

Issues

Are accumulated earnings taxes applicable?

Are income and expense items properly adjusted and accounted for?

Are stock transactions properly accounted for?

Audit Techniques

1. Reconcile income per books with income per return.

2. Reconcile opening balance with year end balance of retained earnings on Schedule M-2.

3. Analyze all increases and decreases.

4. Consider the imposition of Accumulated Earnings Tax (IRC section 531)

This page intentionally left blank.

Chapter 6

EXPENSE ISSUES

GENERAL

Most used car dealerships are owned by one or two people, usually as a sole proprietorship or a corporation. Internal controls tend to be poor at best. The owner(s) treat the business funds as their own, occasionally using these funds to pay for personal expenses. At times these personal expenses are included as business expenses on the books and tax return.

Regardless of the expense account being examined, certain techniques should be applied. Those listed should not preclude using additional techniques should they be warranted. Some of the general techniques that should be used include the following:

1. Reconcile the expense per return to the books.

2. Scan the account and note any large or unusual items, such as payments to the taxpayer's church, political parties, candidates, school tuition, and other personal expenses. Look for items of a capital nature that have a life of more than one year.

3. If an account contains expenditures for gifts or entertainment, review for compliance with IRC section 274.

4. Review questionable checks and receipts or statements, if available, for payments that may be to a political party or candidate, or other personal expenses or capital items.

5. Determine the business purpose behind any material item.

6. Determine the accuracy of accruals.

There are several expense accounts in which issues may be found that apply to all types of businesses. The examination of the advertising, amortization, contributions, dues and subscriptions, legal and professional fees, and employee benefit accounts will not be fully detailed in this manual. Short descriptions of these accounts immediately follow this paragraph.

ADVERTISING EXPENSE

Most used car dealer advertising expenses will be for Yellow Page and newspaper ads. Other common forms of advertising include mailers and sponsorship of recreational sports teams. Some of the larger dealers may also advertise on local radio and television stations. Ads in local church bulletins are a common form of advertising expense that needs to be carefully reviewed.

Taxpayers may occasionally include entertainment expenditures such as tickets to professional sporting events in advertising expense. The record-keeping requirements and limitations of IRC Section 274 apply to these expenditures.

References

IRC Section 162(e)(1) disallows the deductibility of contributions to political candidates or parties.

IRC Section 276 limits the deductibility of advertising expenditures related to political parties.

AMORTIZATION

There is a possibility that a used car dealer will acquire an existing dealership. If an acquisition of assets occurs, goodwill or going concern value may also be acquired. If the taxpayer keeps financial statements, either required by the tax return or a bank or other financial institution, goodwill may be indicated on the balance sheet. Another indication of goodwill is a Schedule M-1 adjustment for a corporate taxpayer.

It is important to analyze any acquisitions. Prior to the Omnibus Reconciliation Act of 1993, the acquisition of goodwill and going concern value were not amortizable for tax purposes. With the enactment of IRC Section 197, the acquisition of goodwill, going-concern value, and other intangibles have a legislated amortizable life of 15 years. IRC section 197 is generally effective after August 10, 1993. There are exceptions to the effective date for binding contracts in existence on August 10, 1993, and a retroactive election for property acquired after July 25, 1991. See Temporary Treas. Reg. section 1.197-1T. IRC section 197 can make it advantageous for taxpayers to value more of the acquisition to intangibles, as opposed to land and buildings. In addition, be alert to the potential overvaluation of inventory and/or short-lived depreciable tangible assets in which taxpayers may seek an even shorter period to recover their investment.

Recent case developments, most notably Newark Morning Ledger Co. v. United States, 507 U.S. 113 S.Ct. 1670 123 L.Ed. 2d. 288 (1993), and the enactment of IRC section 197 have necessitated the revision of outstanding ISP papers on amortization of the following intangible assets:

1. Customer based intangibles,

2. Core deposits,

3. Assembled workforce,

4. Order backlog,

5. Employment contracts,

6. Covenants not to compete,

7. Market based intangibles.

On February 9, 1994, the Service announced a settlement initiative for most of the intangibles issues pending in those years not affected by new Code section 197. The program will not be available for intangibles purchased after July 25, 1991. Because the Service does not believe any return position of taxpayers with respect to the valuation and useful life of intangibles is free from litigation hazards, under the settlement initiative the Service is offering a settlement whereby the taxpayer must agree to the greater of:

1. A minimum of 15 percent disallowance of claimed basis for amortized intangibles, or

2. A 50 ercent cost recovery adjustment for total intangible value.

The 50 percent cost recovery adjustment represents the percentage of total intangibles that must be included in nonamortizable goodwill/going concern value to yield a 50 percent cost recovery at a 5.5 percent discount rate. Under either adjustment, a corresponding adjustment will be made to increase the basis of the nonamortizable goodwill/going concern value. See Intangibles Settlement Initiative Teleconference Handbook, Internal Revenue Service Document 9223 (2-94), Catalog Number 20566N.

Audit Procedures

1. Request schedule to identify assets being amortized.

2. Analyze current year's acquisitions. Analyze prior year acquisitions dependent upon the remaining life and adjusted basis of assets. The Service is not bound by prior accounting methods merely because the tax returns may have been examined and no deficiency was asserted (Lincoln Electric Company v. Commissioner, 71-2 U.S.T.C. P9500 (6th Cir.); Carver v. C.I.R., 173 F.2d 29 (6th Cir. 1949); Fruehauf Corporation v. C.I.R., 356 F.2d 975 (6th Cir. 1966). See Standard Oil Co. (Indiana) v. Commissioner, 77 T.C. 349; and Kilgroe v. United States, 664 F.2d 1168 (10th Cir.) regarding the Service's authority to correct the amount of allowable depreciation deductions in earlier years.

3. Inspect contracts relating to the acquisitions.

4. Determine if any goodwill or going concern value exists, and compare to the values reported. Consider requesting engineering assistance where it appears the taxpayer is under-valuing land and buildings and/or overvaluing inventory and short-lived depreciable tangible assets.5. If an election has been made under IRC section 197, check for compliance with Temporary Treas. Reg. section 1.197-1T.

6. Determine through review of contracts that proper life is being used on amortizable assets.

7. Test check the extensions and proof footings to determine if correct amortization has been computed.

8. Determine if start-up expenses as defined in IRC section 195 have been properly amortized over at least a 60-month period.

CONTRIBUTIONS

Both corporations and sole proprietors may deduct charitable contributions on the return. Corporations may take a limited amount of charitable contributions as a business deduction on Form 1120. However, S-Corporations and partnerships may only show charitable contributions as a deduction on Schedules K and K-1. The sole proprietor can only take the deduction as an itemized deduction on Schedule A, not as a business deduction on Schedule C.

References

IRC section 170 allows charitable contributions as a deduction to corporations and individuals if verified under regulations prescribed by the Secretary. This section also sets limits on the amount that may be deducted and defines what constitutes a charitable contribution.

DUES AND SUBSCRIPTIONS

While examining most used car dealer returns, you will encounter a deduction for dues and subscriptions. This deduction may be shown on the return as dues and subscriptions, or included in other accounts such as other expenses. Most dealers will take deductions for subscriptions to The Kelley Blue Book or similar pricing guidebooks. You will also find subscriptions to various industry magazines and newsletters such as Used Car Merchandising.

Other items a used car dealer may be deducting as dues and subscriptions include membership in local business community organizations such as the Chamber of Commerce. They also may be members of state and local Independent Automobile Dealers Associations as well as the National Independent Automobile Dealers Association.

INTEREST EXPENSE

Most used car dealers will have a line of credit or business loans with a local bank or other financial institution. Most of the loans taken out will be for the purchase of inventory (Flooring).

Sometimes there are miscellaneous interest payments for capital assets, loans from shareholders or personal expenditures. If the taxpayer indicates that a capital asset was purchased, verify that the taxpayer owned the asset. On a corporate return, this can be done through the balance sheet audit approach.

LEGAL AND PROFESSIONAL

Legal fees always deserve a look during the examination. There is always the possibility that personal legal or professional expenses will be paid by the company. Tax preparation fees are a good example. For a sole proprietor, only the portion pertaining to the business is deductible on the Schedule C. See Rev. Rul. 92-29, 1992-1 C.B. 20. For a corporation, any corporate payment for the preparation of the shareholder's return will be disallowed as a deduction to the corporation, and included in gross income as a dividend to the shareholder.

There is the possibility that the taxpayer incurred some legal and professional fees that should be capitalized, such as acquisition fees or start-up costs.

EMPLOYEE BENEFITS

Employee benefits may be a major expense on the tax return. The account can consist of a number of expenses, such as worker's compensation, life insurance, and employee accident and health plans. It may also include expenditures for Christmas parties, company picnics, etc. Since personal expenses can be hidden in some of these items, pay careful attention to anything that appears to benefit the owner.

Audit Procedures

1. Health insurance premiums paid by an S-Corporation for owners of more than 2 percent of the S-Corporation stock are deductible by the corporation, but must also be reported as income to the shareholder. In examining this issue, ensure that the shareholder's Form W-2 includes the value of the premiums paid by the corporation.

2. If the employee benefits account contains gifts to employees, inspect for compliance with the limitations of IRC section 274.

FREIGHT AND DELIVERY

Expenses usually titled freight or delivery are associated with the shipping or delivery of cars or car parts. Costs associated with the delivery of cars should be included in inventory. If these costs are not inventoried, consider proposing an adjustment if the amounts are not de minimis.

If your dealer also repairs cars, freight charges for parts are inventoriable. Any parts in the parts inventory that have not been paid for by the customer should have freight included in their inventoried cost.

Audit Techniques

In addition to the general techniques used to examine all expense issues, the following techniques should be applied:

1. Scan accounts for any material freight and delivery charges. Pay particular attention to expenses incurred at fiscal year.

2. If yearend amounts are material, reconcile these amounts to inventory. If these amounts are not included in inventory, an adjustment should be proposed.

COMMISSIONS AND FEES

Many of the used car dealers will be owner-operated, so commission expenses will not be incurred by the dealer. In cases where the dealer employs salespeople, the salespeople likely will receive commissions which are considered wages and salaries for employment tax purposes from the sales of vehicles. Contracts between employer and employee should specify how commissions wages are determined.

Dealers may also pay commissions or "finder's fees" to other dealers or individuals for locating a specific make or model the dealer needs on his or her lot. Normally, these "finder's fees" are not considered wages since the amount is paid to someone outside the dealer's business. These expenses should be included as part of the inventory costs. A Form 1099 Miscellaneous must be issued if the amount paid to an individual is over $600.

Dealers may incur charges referred to as "hiking" or "shuttling" for the transportation of vehicles. Generally, these expenses are paid to individuals who are hired to drive cars between dealers' lots and to or from auctions. These costs should be inventoried under IRC section 263A if they are associated with moving or shipping property acquired for resale. They also may be subject to employment taxes, depending on the facts and circumstances. See Chapter 7, Required Filing Checks, for additional information concerning employee/independent contractor issue on hiking and portering activities.

Audit Techniques

IRM 4231 and 4233 cover some procedures to consider when examining this issue. These procedures include:

1. Review account and determine that Forms 1099 are being filed when required.

2. Reconcile Forms 1099 issued to Form 1096, Annual Summary and Transmittal to U.S. Information Returns.

3. Determine whether an employer-employee relationship exists for any payments made to individuals that are not treated as wages. Commissions paid to salesmen (employees) are to be included on Forms W-2 along with their salaries.

4. Examine vouchers and determine if commissions represent capital expenditures or inventoriable costs.

5. Examine contracts and determine that commissions are being paid in accordance with contractual obligations.

6. Verify accuracy of accruals.

DEMONSTRATION EXPENSE

Unlike new car dealers, this should not be a significant item. Generally the used car dealer will not have any demo expense. It is most likely that the owner(s) will use the vehicles on the lot for commuting and other personal purposes. If this is the case, corporations should be reporting income on Forms W-2 for the personal use of the cars, and the sole proprietor should be reducing expenses.

The taxpayer may attempt to say that the owner's use of the vehicles is tax free because they qualify as a full-time salesperson under Treas. Reg. section 1.132-5(o). This section defines who is a full-time salesperson, and what is qualified automobile demonstration use.

The taxpayer may also use other arguments to justify using inventory for personal use, such as: he or she had the car repaired and was test-driving the vehicle to make sure the repairs were properly made, or he or she was driving the car around with a for sale sign as advertising. These arguments will have to be addressed on an individual basis, taking into account the facts and circumstances involved.

Audit Techniques

1. Obtain a list of people that used any of the vehicles in inventory, along with the automobiles used.

2. Inquire about the use of the vehicles. Ask for log books. If no logs were kept, ask the taxpayer to reconstruct keeping in mind that Treas. Reg. section 1.274-5(c)(2)(ii)(a) requires that the elements of an expenditure are recorded contemporaneously when the taxpayer has full present knowledge of each element of the expenditure.

3. Check with the Department of Motor Vehicles to verify if the owner of the dealership personally owns any autos. No personal ownership would indicate that he or she uses the business auto for personal purposes.

4. Identify if any values for personal use were included on Forms W-2. If the audit is of a Schedule C, look for a reduction in cost of sales or some other expense to reflect the value of personal use by the owner.

5. There are four acceptable methods of establishing the value placed on personal use of autos owned by the business. Each method is subject to certain requirements,

which will not be detailed in this manual.

6. If it is determined that the annual lease value method should be used, consideration has to be given to what auto value should be applied to the table. If the dealer always uses the most expensive cars on the lot, use an average value of these cars as the annual value. If the owner uses any car on the lot, use the average inventory value as the annual value. If you encounter this issue, obtain a copy of Treas. Reg. section 1.132-5(o), which provides examples for the use of the annual lease value method.

7. The Annual Lease Values do not include the fair market value of fuel provided by the employer, whether fuel is provided in kind or its cost is reimbursed by or charged to the employer. The fuel must be accounted for separately for inclusion in income.

References

IRC section 274(d) -- Substantiation Required.

Treas. Reg. section 1.61-21 provides details on the acceptable methods of establishing the value placed on personal use of automobiles owned by a business. The acceptable methods are:

1. General Method -- Treas. Reg. section 1.61-21(b)(4).

   The general method appears to be based on the assumption that an employee will have only one car available during the course of the year. Under this method, the value of personal use generally is the car's fair market lease value less the portion attributable to business use. It can be very difficult for a dealer to use the general method to determine the value of the employee's personal use of cars during the year.

2. Annual lease value method -- Treas. Reg. section 1.61-21(d).

   Under the annual lease value method, the value of personal use generally is the car's annual lease value less the portion attributable to business use. Annual lease value is intended to reflect the cost of leasing the car for a 4-year term. The rules impose a substantial administrative burden on a dealer when an employee has unrestricted access to more than a few cars during the course of the year.

3. Cents-per-mile value method -- Treas. Reg. section 1.61-21(e) -- Available only in limited circumstances.

4. Commuting value method -- Treas. Reg. section 1.61-21(f) -- Available only in limited circumstances.

Treas. Reg. section 1.132-5(o)(2) defines a "full-time automobile salesman" as any individual who -

1. Is employed by an automobile dealer;

2. Customarily spends at least half of a normal business day performing the functions of a floor sales person or sales manager;

3. Directly engages in substantial promotion and negotiation of sales to customers;

4. Customarily works a number of hours considered full-time in the industry (but at a rate not less than 1,000 hours per year); and

5. Derives at least 25 percent of his/her gross income from the automobile dealership directly as a result of the activities described above.

This section also states "**An individual will not be considered to engage in direct sales activities if the individual's sales related activities are substantially limited to review of sales price offers from customers.** ***[A]n individual who is an owner of the automobile dealership but who otherwise meets the requirements of this paragraph *** may exclude from income the value of qualified automobile demonstrator use. However, the exclusion *** is not available to owners of large automobile dealerships who do not customarily engage in significant sales activities."

INSURANCE EXPENSE

The insurance expense account may consist of several different types of insurance. Typical for a used car dealer would be a multi-line policy for liability and personal property, and a worker's compensation policy. A dealer may also have group medical coverage, group or officer's life insurance, or extended service warranty plans. The larger dealers may also be paying premiums directly or indirectly to a captive offshore insurance company. The New Auto Dealerships Audit Technique Guide provides detailed information concerning the proper treatment of warranty insurance income.

Issues

Numerous issues exist, including:

– deduction of premiums on officer's life insurance,

- deduction of premiums for personal policies,

- self-insurance through a variety of plans, including, but not limited to, producer-owned reinsurance companies, related management companies, and trusts or escrow accounts established by related or unrelated insurance companies, and

- insurance purchased to insure risks under vehicle service contracts.

Audit Techniques

1. Review insurance register and cross reference with fixed assets and inventory.

2. Determine that any non-deductible life insurance premiums were eliminated.

3. Review expense for accuracy of accruals. Big fluctuations should be questioned.

A number of procedures specific to certain issues exist. The procedures are listed below under the issue headings.

Group Health Insurance

Health insurance premiums paid by an S-Corporation for a greater than 2 percent shareholder/employee are deductible by the corporation per IRC section 162(l)(5); and are to be included in the shareholder's gross income per IRC sections 61 and 1372. (See Rev. Rul. 92-16, 1991-1 C.B. 184). The New Auto Dealerships Audit Technique Guide provides detailed information concerning the proper treatment of warranty insurance income. These premiums are not considered wages for social security or Medicare tax purposes. (See Announcement 92-26, 1992-5 Internal Revenue Bulletin 53.)

When examining an S-Corporation, look for this income to be shown on the shareholder's Form 1040. If none is reported, review the policy and premium notices to identify any portion of the premiums applicable to the shareholder. A deduction for 25 percent of health insurance premiums is available for self-employed individuals treated as partners under IRC section 1372. The deduction under IRC section 162(l)(5) was originally scheduled to expire after December 31, 1993. The deduction was extended permanently (retroactive to January 1, 1994), and increased to 30 percent for taxable years beginning after December 31, 1994. (Section 1, Self-Employed Health Insurance Act of 1995, P.L. 104-7 (H.R. 31) signed into law on April 11, 1995.)

Vehicle Service Contracts (Extended Service Warranty)

Used car dealers sell two basic types of extended service contracts. The first type is between the customer and an unrelated underwriter. The dealer is merely an agent for the underwriter and keeps as profit the difference between the sales price of the contract and the "cost" paid to the underwriter.

The second type is a contract between the customer and the dealer. For this type the dealer may buy insurance covering his or her risk or be "self-insured." If the dealer buys insurance, the income and expenses should be reported according to Rev. Proc. 92-97 and/or 92-98. The Government's position is that all of the income must be reported in the year of receipt, and any prepaid insurance must be amortized over the life of the policy under IRC section 167(a) and Treas. Reg. section 1.167(a)-3.

The taxpayer can elect to mitigate this situation by filing Form 3115 to request changes in accounting methods. Rev. Proc. 92-97 and Reve. Proc. 92-98 explain the filing procedures, which allow taxpayers to report income ratably as they expense the insurance ratably.

While interviewing the taxpayer, ask about extended service warranties. If the taxpayer sells warranties, determine if they are primarily liable for any warranty, or if they just act as an agent. (You may have to read the actual contracts to determine who is the obligor.) If the taxpayer is primarily liable, ask if elections to change accounting methods were filed.

Corporate Owned Life Insurance

The emerging issue of "leveraged corporate owned life insurance" has been identified. The issue has been found in both large corporate examinations and small corporations that employ the primary shareholders. The small corporation cases typically involve a life insurance product known as a "split-dollar" life insurance policy owned by the employer or a key person life insurance policy owned by the corporation. In the split dollar cases, the corporation may be claiming interest deductions on debt from the insurance company used to pay a premium to the insurance company. In reality, however, these interest payments may be more properly characterized as premium paid on behalf of the employer, thereby producing taxable income to the employee. See Young v. Commissioner, T.C. Memo. 1995-379. Any adjustments for this type of insurance would be a disallowance of interest deduction to the corporation and an increase of income to the shareholder(s). The interest paid on debt used to purchase key person insurance may be generated by the same "loan premium" transaction that might also be non-deductible under a similar sham loan analysis.

When examining the issue, it is necessary to determine the nature of all interest payments deducted on the return. If any interest is attributable to a loan from an insurance company, further inquiries should be made concerning the transaction to determine if the interest payment is actually a disguised insurance premium payment. If this type of issue is found or suspected, the examiner should contact the issue specialist for corporate owned life insurance ("COLI").

PAYROLL

Payroll should be examined in relation to the returns filing checks for employment taxes. In the audit of a new car dealer, an agent will often find in the vicinity of 8 to 10 separate payroll accounts, in addition to yearend adjusting entries. Used car dealers will not have as complex a system.

Often times, dealers will include some of the payroll in cost of goods sold. You need to be aware of this when reconciling payroll from the employment tax returns to the income tax return. If you can not easily reconcile the two, have the taxpayer reconcile the difference for you.

Reconciling the employment tax returns to the income tax return will serve the purpose of identifying who was treated as an employee. This will prove helpful when an employee versus independent contractor issue arises, since you will know everyone who was treated as an employee.

Audit Techniques

1. As part of package audit procedures, reconcile employment tax returns to transcripts.

2. Scan non-payroll accounts such as "legal and professional fees," "repairs and maintenance," or "other expenses" for employment tax issues.

POLICY WORK OR ADJUSTMENTS

The expenses charged to these accounts are for the vehicle repairs which are not covered under the automobile's standard warranty or an extended service warranty. The dealer will pay for these expenses to create goodwill or sustain good customer relations.

Audit Technique

Scan the ledgers for material items, looking for payments made for autos owned by the owner or his/her relatives or employees.

RENT EXPENSE

In many cases, used car dealerships do not own the building and lot from which they conduct their business activities. In the case of corporations, the shareholder often owns the property and rents to the corporation. Frequently, the owners of sole proprietorships will own the building and lot from which they operate the business.

When dealing with the rental issue on Schedules C, you need to be aware of the Cox case, T. C. Memo. 1993-326 (below). In this case, the spouse owning a business that pays rent to the couple was allowed a deduction of one-half of the rent as a business expense, even when filing a joint return.

In addition to paying rent, a lease may require a lessee to pay specified expenses of the lessor. Such leases, commonly referred to as "net leases" or "care-free leases," may require the lessee to pay expenses including the lessor's real estate taxes or insurance premiums. Treas. Reg. section 1.61-8(c) treats these payments as additional "constructive" rent payments between the lessee and the lessor. Treas. Reg. section 1.162-11(a) provides: "Taxes paid by a tenant to or for a landlord for business property are additional *** income to the landlord, the amount of tax being deductible by the latter." The same treatment is accorded insurance premiums and other deductible expenses of the landlord that are paid by the tenant. The treatment accorded the landlord depends on the landlord's method of accounting and whether the expenses are paid directly by the tenant/lessee or paid to the landlord/lessor.

If the lessor is a related party owning more than 50 percent of the lessee by attribution, IRC section 267(a)(2) must be considered. This section applies when the lessee is on the accrual basis and the lessor is on the cash basis of accounting. It requires a matching of income and expense, thus the lessor and the lessee are treated as if both are on the cash basis. In this case, no expense deduction, in advance of payment, is allowable. IRC section 267 overrides IRC section 461. Remember the expense is rent even though the lessee may deduct it as taxes, insurance, etc.

Issues

In the case of a corporation, are rental payments actually a disguised dividend?

Is the amount paid at or above fair rental value?

Is the owner paying himself rent to avoid self-employment taxes?

Are real estate taxes accrued by a lessee relating to a "net lease" deductible?

Audit Techniques

1. Review account to determine reason for any fluctuations.

2. Examine lease agreements and determine if correctly reflected.

3. Determine reasonableness of rents paid to related parties.

4. Determine accuracy of accruals.

References

D. S. Cox, T.C. Memo 1993-326, allows a married couple that filed a joint return and owned property as tenants by the entirety to include as income on Schedule E one half of the rent received from the husband's sole proprietorship. They were also entitled to deduct one half of the rent paid by the husband's business as a Schedule C business expense. The amount allowed as a deduction was considered to be his wife's portion of the rental income and expense. His portion of the rent expense on the Schedule C was not allowed as a deduction and was not included on Schedule E. The opinion has been issued, however, the decision has not been entered. The Internal Revenue Service is considering an appeal of this case, but no final decision has been made by the National Office at this time.

TRAVEL AND ENTERTAINMENT

Travel and entertainment (T&E) is always an area of concern. Common forms of abuse include travel to national and state association meetings by the owners' family members when there is no business requirement that they attend the meetings, taking family members on buying trips to line up purchase of cars, and meals for family members. You may also find tickets to professional sporting events included in this account. **NOTE: The 80 percent limitation on meals and entertainment has been reduced to 50 percent for years beginning after 1993.**

IRC sections 162 and 274 provide the requirements that must be met for travel and entertainment expenses. Failure to meet these requirements means no deduction for the taxpayer, and possibly constructive dividends for a corporate shareholder.

Audit Techniques

1. IRM 4231-5(10)(16)0 suggests some guidelines to follow while examining Travel and Entertainment. Two of these are discussed in paragraphs a and b below.

   a. Cash expenditures and checks payable to owners and employees closely related by blood or marriage to the owners, should be closely examined as to the actual payment of the expenditures and the business purpose.

   b. Although prizes and awards are not prevalent in the used car industry, during the initial interview examiners should determine whether prize or contest awards in any form of remuneration have been made to an individual. If the recipient of the prize or award is an individual other than an employee of the business making the award, the examiner should ascertain whether proper Forms 1099 have been filed reporting the amount of money or fair market value of the prize or award given to each recipient. If Forms 1099 required to be filed have not been filed, the procedures in IRM 4562.5 should be followed.

   c. Cash and noncash prizes or awards made to an employee by, or on behalf of, an employer are considered wages, and as such, should be included on an employee's Form W-2. Certain length of service and safety awards are excluded from FICA taxes if the provisions of IRC sections 74(c), 274(j), and 3121(a)(20) are met. There are additional exceptions for such things as Christmas turkeys, etc.

2. The new auto dealership text refers to the 80 percent limitation to meals and entertainment for years ending in 1987. On corporate returns, there should be a Schedule M-1 adjustment reflecting the limitation. The Schedule C has a separate line to reflect the adjustment. If there are no entries of this type on either return, an adjustment is necessary. Remember that if an adjustment is made to reduce the deductible expense, an adjustment to reduce the limitation amount also is necessary. See Note above.

3. The SAIN audit procedures, numbers 526-07 and 526-08 of IRM 4233 provide the following procedure to consider.

   – Determine if "sales conventions" and "meetings" have a business purpose or whether they are in fact employer paid vacations.

<u>References</u>

IRC section 274(d)

SUBSTANTIATION REQUIRED. -- No deduction or credit shall be allowed--

* * * * * * *

unless the taxpayer substantiates by adequate records or by sufficient evidence corroborating the taxpayer's own statement (A) the amount of such expense or other item, (B) the time and place of the travel, entertainment, amusement, recreation or use of the facility of property, or the date and description of the gift, (C) the business purpose of the expense or other item and (D) the business relationship to the taxpayers of persons entertained, using the facility or property or receiving the gift. ***

This page intentionally left blank.

Chapter 7

REQUIRED FILING CHECKS

GENERAL INFORMATION

Part of the standard examination for all types of business activities consists of the required filing checks. Agents should be aware of these procedures; therefore, this section will emphasize those issues pertaining specifically to independent used car dealers.

The following forms should be inspected as part of the returns filing checks.

Forms	Notes
W-4	Check for unusually large number of dependents or exemptions from withholding. Follow up with inspection of Forms W-2 as necessary.
W-2	Scrutinize all Forms W-2 for any withholding which appears to be small in relationship to the wages reported. If an employment tax audit is warranted the W-2 information will be needed to determine if the FUTA and FICA limitations have been met. In many cases, the FUTA limit will have been met, but the FICA limit will not have been met. **Be aware that the ceiling on the Hospital Insurance portion of FICA was eliminated effective January 1, 1994.**
1099	Consider the issue of employee vs. independent contractor, particularly if outside individuals are used for shuttling and portering activities. Discussed in detail later in this section.
940 and 941	Issues may include employer/independent contractor status of hikers (shuttlers) and other outside workers (discussed later in this section) as well as personal use of business autos by employees. See Chapter 6, Expense Issues, on Demonstrators for detailed information.

1040	Constructive dividends, flow through items from partnership and S-corporation returns. Spouse's return if married, filing separately.
8300	Currency transactions over $10,000. The review of these forms should be conducted in conjunction with the auditof the cash accounts.
5500 and 5500C	Review pension expenses and distributions. See Chapter 6, Expense Issues, dealing with Employee Benefits for a brief discussion of pensions and other benefits.

Other items that need to be considered as a part of the required filing checks include:

Bartering	Consider along with the audit of income accounts. Some used car dealers in some parts of the country have been found to belong to bartering clubs. See the Chapter 3, Gross Receipts, for more information.
Political Contributions	Consider these in conjunction with auditing contributions and dues and subscriptions. See Chapter 6, Expense Issues, dealing with Contributions and Dues and Subscriptions for details.
Inventory Checks	See Chapter 4, Cost of Goods Sold/Inventory, for details of inventory issues and techniques.
Excise Tax Returns	Examiners are required to determine if the taxpayer has met the filing requirements for Federal excise tax.

FORM 8300

Required filing checks include inspecting for cash transactions over $10,000. Cash receipts must be examined to determine if all necessary Forms 8300 (Currency Transaction Report Over $10,000) have been properly filed. If delinquent Forms 8300 exist, then penalties must be considered and the Revenue Agent's Report must have a comment regarding compliance and application or nonapplication of penalties.

References

IRC section 6050I(a)

(a) CASH RECEIPTS OF MORE THAN $10,000. -- Any Person-

    (1) who engaged in a trade or business, and

    (2) who, in the course of such trade or business, receives more than $10,000 in cash in 1 transaction (or 2 or more related transactions),

shall make the return described in subsection (b) with respect to such transaction (or related transactions) at such time as the Secretary may by regulations prescribe.

Treas. Reg. section 1.6050I-1(c)(1)(ii) details the reporting requirements for single and multiple payments.

Extract

Treas. Reg. section 1.6050I-1(c)(1)(ii)

  (ii) *** For amounts received on or after February 3, 1992, the term "cash" means--

    (A) The coin and currency of the United States or any other country, which circulate in and are customarily used and accepted as money in the country in which issued; and

    (B) A cashier's check (by whatever name called, including "treasurer's check" and "bank check"), bank draft, traveler's check, or money order having a face value amount of not more than $10,000 -

        (1) Received in a designated reporting transaction as defined in paragraph (c)(1)(iii) of this section (except as provided in paragraphs (c)(1)(iv), (v), and (vi) of this section), or

        (2) Received in any transaction in which the recipient knows that such instrument is being used in an attempt to avoid the reporting of the transaction under section 6050I and this section.

EMPLOYEE/INDEPENDENT CONTRACTOR STATUS

Employment taxes can amount to a significant tax liability. The treatment of drivers (also known as hikers or shuttlers), salesmen/buyers, and porters as independent contractors should not be overlooked during the audit of retail or wholesale used car dealers and brokers.

Most dealers will pay salesmen a commission based on sales. There usually will be a written contract stating how the amount of commission will be determined. The majority of used car dealers will treat salesmen as employees for tax purposes; however, some dealers will treat their salesmen as independent contractors. Revenue Rulings have determined car salesmen are employees whose commissions are subject to FICA, FUTA, and Federal tax withholding requirements.

Some dealers find individuals, called porters, who will clean the autos before resale. Many of these porters will earn less than $600, so you may find no Forms 1099 filed on behalf of these people if they are treated as independent contractors. Regardless of the amount earned, if they are treated as employees, a Form W-2 should be filed. These individuals may or may not be employees based on facts and circumstances.

Many used car dealers will pay individuals to drive cars to the dealer's lot, auto auctions, or other dealers' lots. The drivers may be used on a regular or sporadic basis throughout the year. While some dealers may hire a friend or relative to drive the autos for no more than the cost of a meal, most dealers use outside individuals and pay them with a check or cash. These individuals may be employees or independent contractors, based on facts and circumstances of each case.

In many larger cities, there are various companies that will supply drivers to used car dealers who are in need of having cars shuttled from one location to another. These drivers are not treated as employees of the car dealer as the drivers are employees of the company providing the services.

Buyers or brokers may be employees or independent contractors. The facts and circumstances will be the determining factor. For example some buyers or brokers will work for several dealers while others will work exclusively for one dealer.

Issue

Are the drivers and porters independent contractors or employees?

Audit Techniques

During the initial interview, question the owner about individuals from outside the business such as porters and hikers. It is essential that you determine the source of these individuals. There are companies that will provide drivers or porters to dealers and others in the community. If the dealer is getting his or her drivers and porters from such an organization, usually the drivers are controlled by the provider company and are treated as its employees. If they are not controlled by a provider company, they are probably employees of the dealer. (See Revenue Ruling 66-381, 1966-2 C.B. 449.)

If the dealer is not using another company to provide drivers and porters, you may have an employment tax issue. The initial interview should provide you with the necessary information to determine if there is an issue. The usual common law rules should be applied as soon as it appears that there is an independent contractor/employee issue. While no one factor is dominant, control or the right to control the performance of duties plays a large role in the determination of whether an individual is an employee or independent contractor.

The following is a brief outline of the law regarding employment status and employment tax relief. It is important to note that either worker classification -- independent contractor or employee -- can be a valid and appropriate business choice. For an in-depth discussion, see the training materials on determining employment status. "Independent Contractor or Employee?" Training 3320-102 (Rev. 10-96) TPDS 84238I. The training materials are also available from the IRS Home Page (http://www.irs.ustreas.gov).

The first step in any case involving worker classification is to consider section 530. Section 530 of the Revenue Act of 1978 was enacted by Congress to provide relief to certain taxpayers who had acted in good faith in classifying their workers from the potentially harsh retroactive tax liabilities resulting from IRS reclassification of independent contractors as employees. The statute is a relief provision and provides an alternative method by which to avoid employment tax liability where a taxpayer cannot establish his workers are or were independent contractors.

In order to qualify for section 530 relief, the business must meet consistency and reasonable basis tests. The consistency test requires that the business has filed all required Forms 1099 with respect to the worker for the period, on a basis consistent with treatment of the worker as not being an employee (reporting consistency); and that the business has treated all workers in similar positions the same (substantive consistency).

Under the reasonable basis test, the business must have had some reasonable basis for not treating the worker as an employee. There are three "safe harbors" that form the basis for an objective reasonable basis standard under section 530. These safe harbors are: (1) judicial precedent, published rulings, technical advice to the taxpayer or a letter ruling to the taxpayer; (2) a past favorable IRS audit on the same issue; and (3) long-standing, recognized practice of a significant segment of the industry in which the individual was engaged. A business that fails to meet any of these three safe havens may still be entitled to relief if it can demonstrate that it relied on some other reasonable basis for not treating a worker as an employee.

Before or at the beginning of any audit inquiry relating to employment status, an agent must provide the taxpayer with a written notice of the provisions of section 530. If the requirements of section 530 are met, a business may be entitled to relief from federal employment tax obligations. Section 530 terminates the business's, not the worker's employment tax liability and any interest or penalties attributable to the liability for employment taxes.

In general, the common law rules are applied in determining the employer-employee relationship. Internal Revenue Code section 3121 (d) (2). Nationwide Mutual Insurance Co. V. Darden, 503 U.S. 318 (1992).

Guides for determining a worker's employment status are found in three substantially similar sections of the Employment Tax Regulations; namely, sections 31.3121(d)-1, 31.3306(i)-1, and 31.3401(c)-1, relating to the Federal Insurance Contributions Act (FICA), the Federal Unemployment Tax Act (FUTA), and federal income tax withholding, respectively.

The regulations provide that, generally, the relationship of employer and employee exists when the person for whom the services are performed has the right to control and direct the individual who performs the services not only as to the result to be accomplished by the work but also as to the details and means by which that result is accomplished. The examiner will need to weigh the facts and circumstances of each case and determine worker status accordingly.

The training materials provide more information on the method of analysis used in determining employment status. They explain the kinds of facts to be considered, including those evidencing behavioral control, those evidencing financial control, and those evidencing the relationship of the parties.

For further assistance regarding employment tax issues, contact the employment coordinator.

It is important that you discuss the reasons workers were treated as independent contractors with the taxpayer as early as possible in the examination process. Keep notes of the taxpayer's responses during the discussion. A taxpayer cannot have relied on recently decided cases for years prior to the taxpayer's decision. An opinion letter from an attorney written after the examination began is less persuasive than one written when the taxpayer first began using the workers and treating them as independent contractors.

REFERENCES

IRC section 3301 imposes on every employer for each calendar year an excise tax, with respect to having individuals in his or her employ, equal to 6.2 percent of the total wages paid during the calendar year.

IRC section 3101(a) imposes a tax on the income of every individual for Old-Age, Survivors, and Disability Insurance.

IRC section 3101(b) imposes a tax on the income of every individual for Hospital Insurance.

IRC section 3509 provides a "statutory offset mechanism that apply in reclassification cases." If any employer fails to deduct and withhold any income or social security tax by reason of treating an employee as an independent contractor, IRC section 3509 provides different rates for determining an employer's employment tax liability. The employer pays the full amount of the employer's share of FICA and FUTA taxes. However, IRC section 3509 provides a reduced rate for the employees' FICA tax and their income tax liability.

Employment Tax Regulations sections 31.3121(d)-1, 31.3306(i)-1, and 31.3401(c)-1 relate to the FICA, the FUTA, and Federal income tax withholding, respectively.

Section 31.3121(d)-2 requires the application of the common law rules in determining the employer-employee relationship.

Rev. Rul. 72-74, 1972-1 C.B. 318 states that when an individual engages in the wholesale purchase and sales of used cars between licensed dealers for a company that does not have the right to control his or her business operations, he or she is not an employee of the company.

Avis Rent A Car System, Inc., 503 F.2d 423 (2d Cir. 1974), an auto rental company was denied a refund of FICA, FUTA, and income withholding taxes paid on behalf of shuttlers since the shuttlers were employees and not independent contractors.

Rev. Rul. 73-260, 1973-1 C.B. 412 details the method of determining wages of an agent or commissioned driver who is an employee for FICA and FUTA purposes.

Neely, T.C. Memo 1978-18, in applying the common-law tests to determine an employer-employee relationship, the evidence established the taxpayer, a used car salesman, was an employee.

Rev. Rul. 55-144, 1955-1 C.B. 483 states that an individual employed by a used car dealer to drive cars to an auction company located in a city distant from the dealer's place of business, instructed with respect to the price at which the cars are to be sold at auction, required to protect that price, paid all expenses of the trip, and remunerated on the basis of a stated amount for each car sold, is an employee of the dealer.

Rev. Rul. 69-349, 1969-1 C.B. 261 states that drivers are employees where the company exercises control as to the details and manner of performance of services.

Exhibits 7-1 and 7-2 are sample workpapers taken from examinations involving the employee/independent contractor issue. The responses shown are intended to be samples of possible responses provided by taxpayers. Not all factors will apply to all cases. The examiner has the responsibility to determine what applies to the facts and circumstances of each case and make a determination on those facts and circumstances.

Exhibit 7-1 (1 of 3)

SAMPLE WORK PAPER

19XX 940 - 941'S
20 COMMON LAW FACTORS

1. **INSTRUCTIONS:**
When needed, drivers are instructed by corporate officers/ employees as to where and when cars are to be picked up and delivered and whom to contact when the driver arrives at the pickup and/or delivery location.

2. **TRAINING:**
No special training is required.

3. **INTEGRATION:**
Transportation of used cars from one location to another is an essential part of the wholesale used car business. Success of the business depends on getting cars to the retail dealers at the right time. The use of drivers is essential to meet this requirement.

4. **SERVICES RENDERED PERSONALLY:**
Driving services are rendered personally and the dealer has interest in the methods used and the results of the transfer of the cars from one location to another.

5. **HIRING, SUPERVISING, AND PAYING ASSISTANTS:**
All drivers are paid by the taxpayer. No payments are made to or by a middleman.

6. **CONTINUING RELATIONSHIP:**
The same individuals were used in all 3 years examined. Several of the drivers earned substantial amounts, indicating they were frequent drivers. This indicates a continuing relationship.

7. **SET HOURS OF WORK:**
The corporation sets the times when the drivers are needed to transport used cars.

8. **FULL TIME REQUIRED:**
Full time is not required for this job. The drivers work when available.

9. **DOING WORK ON EMPLOYER'S PREMISES:**
Cars may be picked up from or delivered to the business location or they may be picked up from and delivered to other dealers. Work is done not at the physical location of the dealership, but in cars owned by the dealership.

NAME:
YEAR: AGENT:
DATE: PAGE:

Exhibit 7-1 (2 of 3)

SAMPLE WORK PAPER

19XX 940 - 941'S
20 COMMON LAW FACTORS

10. **ORDER OR SET SEQUENCE:**
The worker picks up the vehicle at the location prescribed by the dealer and delivers it to the required location. The order or sequence is determined by the duties (moving vehicles from one location to another).

11. **ORAL OR WRITTEN REPORTS:**
The driver does not report directly back to the dealer. The purchasing dealer returns a copy of the assigned title to the seller which verifies accomplishment of the delivery. If the car is involved in an accident, the driver notifies the dealer for which he or she is driving.

12. **PAYMENT BY THE HOUR, WEEK OR MONTH:**
Drivers are paid by the trip.

13. **PAYMENT OF BUSINESS AND/OR TRAVELING EXPENSES:**
The corporation pays the drivers for expenses such as gas and oil for the cars and tolls. The drivers are not paid for meals when driving.

14. **FURNISHING OF TOOLS OR MATERIALS:**
All materials (cars) are furnished by the corporation. The drivers are providing only their driving skills.

15. **SIGNIFICANT INVESTMENT:**
The corporation has a significant investment in the purchase of used cars. The corporation also has a significant investment in the insurance coverage on the cars while being shuttled from one location to another. The drivers have no investment involved.

16. **REALIZATION OF PROFIT OR LOSS:**
The company can realize a profit or loss, whereas the drivers are reimbursed for expenses other than meals. The drivers do not realize any risk of losses as they are reimbursed for their expenses.

17. **WORKING FOR MORE THAN ONE FIRM AT A TIME:**
The drivers have the opportunity to work for more than one dealer or may work other jobs on a full or part-time basis.

18. **MAKING SERVICES AVAILABLE TO THE GENERAL PUBLIC:**
The drivers offered their services to several dealerships. Several dealers used the same drivers based on dealer recommendations. Aside from working for other dealers, it was not known if the drivers made themselves available to the general public.

NAME: _____
YEAR: _____ AGENT: _____
DATE: _____ PAGE: _____

Exhibit 7-1 (3 of 3)

SAMPLE WORK PAPER

19XX 940 - 941'S
20 COMMON LAW FACTORS

19. **RIGHT TO DISCHARGE:**
   The corporation has the right to discharge or not to use a driver if the corporation finds the drivers not performing their duties.

20. **RIGHT TO TERMINATE:**
   The drivers have the right to terminate their relationship with the corporation at any time.

Based on the above application of the Twenty Common Law Factors, _____, Inc. has the right to control the workers involved in shuttling cars on a part-time basis. The workers, because of the dealer's right to control their actions in performance of their duties, are employees of the dealer.

NAME: _____
YEAR: _____ AGENT: _____
DATE: _____ PAGE: _____

This page intentionally left blank.

Exhibit 7-2 (1 of 2)

Form 886-A	EXPLANATION OF ITEMS	Schedule No., or Exhibit
Name of Taxpayer		Year/Period

FICA/WITHHOLDING	/ /	/ /	/ /
PER RETURN:	$	$	$
PER AUDIT:	$	$	$
ADJUSTMENT	$	$	$
FUTA	/ /	/ /	/ /
PER RETURN:	$	$	$
PER AUDIT:	$	$	$
ADJUSTMENT:	$	$	$

ISSUE: Are drivers subject to Employment Taxes (FICA & FUTA)?

FACTS:

_____, used outside drivers to shuttle cars from one location to another. These drivers are used on an as needed basis. The corporation provides insurance coverage on the drivers while cars are being shuttled. Drivers are also reimbursed for gas, oil, and tolls incurred while driving for the corporation. _____ calls the drivers when needed and has the right to reject any driver sent over. Payments are made directly to the drivers. The person supplying the drivers receives no payment unless actually driving.

LAW:

IRC section 3301 imposes on every employer for each calendar year an excise tax, with respect to having individuals in his or her employ, equal to 6.2 percent of the total wages paid during the calendar year.

IRC section 3101(a) imposes a tax on the income of every individual for Old-Age, Survivors, and Disability Insurance.

IRC section 3101(b) imposes a tax on the income of every individual for Hospital Insurance.

IRC section 3509(a) imposes on the employer an additional 20 percent FICA when employees are treated not being an employee. It also imposes withholding at 1.5 percent of the wages paid to such employees

Exhibit 7-2 (2 of 2)

Form 886-A	EXPLANATION OF ITEMS	Schedule No., or Exhibit
Name of Taxpayer		Year/Period

Employment Tax Regulations section 3121(d)(2) requires the application if the common law rules in determining the employer-employee relationship.

Rev. Rul. 69-349, 1969-1 C.B. 261 determined that drivers were employees where a company exercised control as to details and manner of services.

Rev. Rul. 55-144, 1955-1 C.B. 483 determined that individuals employed by a used car dealer to drive cars to auction in another city and were given instructions with respect to price, paid all expenses of the trip and remunerated on the basis of a stated amount for each car sold, are employees of that used car dealer.

Avis Rent A Car System, Inc., 503 F.2d 423 (2d Cir. 1974) determined that car shuttlers were employees subject to FICA and FUTA taxes, and not independent contractors.

CONCLUSION:

The corporation reimburses the drivers for expenses such as tolls and gas. Such reimbursement is typical of an employer-employee relationship. Independent contractors are not normally reimbursed for expenses, but deduct them on their tax returns.

The corporation sets the hours of work and takes the financial risks if the vehicles are not delivered in good condition. The corporation provides instructions as to when and where vehicles are to be picked up and delivered. All necessary materials (cars) are provided by the dealer. The dealer also provides insurance coverage for the cars and drivers while cars are being transported from one location to another.

Based on the above factors, the corporation has the right to and does exercise a certain amount of control over the activities performed by the drivers in question. Such control indicates an employer/employee relationship as defined by Rev. Rul. 69-349. Based on the information provided by _____, President of the corporation, and the application of the Common Law Rules and the 20 Common Law Factors (Exhibit 7-1), the drivers are employees.

The *Avis Rent A Car* case and Revenue Rulings cited above further support the determination that the drivers used by the corporation are employees, and should be treated as such for FICA and FUTA taxes. Adjustments to the Forms 940 and 941 are made as shown above under provisions of IRC sections 3101(a) for FICA and IRC section 3301 for FUTA.

Chapter 8

RELATED FINANCE COMPANIES

OVERVIEW

The use of related finance companies (RFC) is a common practice in the used car industry. Such companies serve many valid business purposes and were utilized before any tax advantage scheme was offered. However, some RFC's are being utilized by used and new car dealers to reduce or defer the reporting of income. This section of the guide is to be used as an overview of RFC's. In it will be found reasons for establishing RFC's, and issues faced in the examination of a RFC issue.

There are three issues that exist in dealing with RFC's. The first involves the economic reasons for the arrangement, the second involves the validity (form) of the RFC itself, and the third and most critical issue involves the economic substance of the discounting transactions.

ECONOMIC REASONS

There are several reasons for creating and using a RFC. The following are some of the major reasons that a RFC is created. Each of these reasons can provide a significant and valid business and economic reason for creating a separate entity to finance the dealer's receivables, even if no third party receivables are acquired. There are others that are equally valid and legitimate reasons for using a RFC.

1. Providing credit to enable the purchaser to buy a car.

    Many, if not most of the purchasers that utilize the services of a RFC do so because of an inability to get credit elsewhere. In this way the RFC serves a useful purpose in providing credit to individuals with little, no, or bad credit. A properly operating RFC also focuses the collection function outside of the dealership itself, which relieves the sales personnel from a task that is time consuming. Payment schedules are on a weekly or monthly basis.

2. Improving the collection of accounts receivable.

    A RFC can significantly enhance the collection of accounts receivable by requiring the borrower/buyer to remit payments to a third party, even though the third party is related to the dealer. It has been the industry's experience that when payment is

8-1

made directly to the dealer, a bad experience with the car often leads to a default on the note for the car. This, in turn, creates a collection problem, and possibly a publicity problem for the dealership. On the other hand, if a RFC is involved, experience shows that the customer is less likely to default on the payment. Given the general credit worthiness of the customers, this is a significant advantage. Some dealers, through effective management and controls, have RFC discount rates lower than what they can obtain from third parties and still make a profit on their RFC financing operations.

3. Avoiding licensing and other regulatory requirements on the dealer entity.

    Many states have licensing requirements for finance companies. Establishing a RFC permits the dealer to isolate liability for violation of any requirements in a separate entity, without jeopardizing the status of the dealership. In addition, some states have capital requirements for finance companies that may interfere with the normal operations of a dealership.

4. Preventing adverse publicity on repossessions and other collection actions from affecting the dealership.

    Repossession and collection problems are a daily fact of life for buy here/pay here dealers. Creation of a RFC permits a new entity to undertake these actions, thereby insulating the dealer from any adverse publicity. Even in states where disclosure of the relationship is required, the resulting publicity is usually less adverse when a RFC is used.

5. Insulating the dealership from the financial risk of default on the notes.

    The industry deals with a customer base that generally has poor or non-existent credit. The default rate on buy here/pay here notes is substantially higher than on general bank loans. This economic fact is recognized both by the interest rates charged by the dealer or finance company and the reserves that independent finance companies generally maintain. A separate RFC removes the financial risk from the dealership entity.

6. Diversification of ownership.

    Since the financing of used cars is not inherently a part of a dealership, a RFC permits the dealer to provide ownership in that specific business to both family and non-family members without diluting ownership in the dealership. This allows the dealer to separate the two businesses and reward certain employees or other individuals with an ownership interest in a segment of the business.

A final advantage is that a RFC can be expanded, depending upon the dealer's desire, to finance unrelated receivables as well as those of a particular dealership. It should be pointed out that although this is possible, it rarely happens.

VALIDITY OR FORM OF RFC

The second issue that should be considered, the form issue, is how a valid RFC is structured and operated. Since the purpose of the RFC is to isolate liability or segregate transactions in a separate entity, the RFC should meet several criteria to be treated as a separate, valid business. These criteria are:

1. The RFC should be a separate, legal entity.

2. The RFC should meet all licensing requirements of the jurisdictions in which it operates.

3. A major factor is that the RFC should be adequately capitalized in order to pay for the contracts.

4. The RFC should have its own employees and compensate them directly. However, the fact that the RFC and the dealership or other related entities may elect to use a common paymaster does not indicate, in any way, that the RFC does not have its own employees.

5. The RFC should obtain and maintain all appropriate local business and similar licenses.

6. The RFC should have a separate telephone number.

7. The RFC should have a separate business address, which may be a post office box. Even if a separate business address is maintained, it is common for the RFC to have an office at the dealership.

8. The RFC should maintain a separate set of books and records.

9. The RFC should comply with all title, lien, and recordation rules in the jurisdictions in which it operates.

10. The RFC should notify customers of the purchase of their notes.

11. The RFC and the dealership should have a purchase contract for the receivables that both complies with the appropriate state law and provides evidence of how the FMV of the receivables was determined.

12. The RFC should pay the dealer for the receivables at the time of purchase. The RFC can generate the cash to make the payment from any combination of capitalization of the RFC, bank or third party borrowings, or borrowings from related entities or shareholders. Borrowings from related entities or shareholders can diminish the validity of this factor.

13. The RFC should be operated in a business-like

Clearly, to the extent that these attributes are absent, a serious question as to the substance of the RFC exists.

ECONOMIC SUBSTANCE

The third and most important issue that should be addressed is the sale of discounted receivables at fair market value (FMV). Sales of receivables must have economic substance to qualify for tax purposes; valid business reasons alone will not suffice.

The FMV of a receivable or group of receivables will depend on a number of factors, the facts and circumstances of each receivable determining the importance of each factor. Purchasing receivables is not an exact science, and many subjective factors enter into the determination of value. The industry's position is that a deep discount is warranted in nearly all transfers of receivables. The factors that directly influence the amount of discount include:

1. Absence of or poor credit history.

2. History of payments on the note.

3. Amount of time left on the note.

4. The age of the vehicle.

Reviews of some third-party finance company documents indicate that these companies can offer to acquire the receivables from dealers at up to a 50 percent up-front discount. These discounts apply whether or not the finance company buys in bulk or "cherry picks" the best accounts.

It is also important to note that these same third-party finance company documents refer to back-end reserves. These back-end reserves can be released to the dealer at the time the loan is paid off. The back-end reserves can restore the dealers profit on the sale to 100 percent, less any transaction costs. RFC purchases at a deep discount should be inspected for these back-end reserves.

A dealer can use a RFC to discount it's receivables and have it accepted for tax purposes. To summarize the above discussion, the following three factors need to be addressed:

1. The discounting transactions must have economic substance. All of the relevant facts and circumstances must be considered. Remember that the primary reasons for selling receivables are to obtain cash (improve cash flow) or to shift risk. If both of these are missing, it is a good indication that the sales transaction lack economic substance.

2. The form of the transactions and the form of the RFC must be perfected.

3. The receivables must be sold for fair market value. The seller and purchaser must base the discount on some reasonable factors, not on an arbitrary determination of the discount rate.

ISSUES

Related finance company transactions such as the example above may raise several issues. Among the issues that may arise are the following:

1. Whether there has been a change in method of accounting where a related refinance company is used to defer income.

2. Whether a loss incurred by a car dealer from the purported sale of notes receivable to a related finance company should be disallowed because the related finance company existed only in form and the transaction between the dealer and related finance company lacks economic substance.

3. Whether IRC section 482 applies to the loss claimed by a dealer from the sale of notes receivable to a related finance company because the notes receivable were sold at less than the fair market value amount.

4. Whether Internal Revenue Code Section 267 disallows a loss from the sale of notes receivable by a car dealer to a related finance company.

5. Whether a dealer and related finance company are members of a controlled group for the purposes of IRC section 267, and thereby eligible for the special loss recognition rules of Treas. Reg. section 1.267(f)-1(f).

ISSUE DEVELOPMENT

Issue development is the key to any substance versus form argument. This is especially true when related corporations are involved. Depending on the facts and circumstances of each dealership, the RFC could be a valid business and should be respected as a separate entity. Your issue will be resolved based on the particular facts and circumstances of your taxpayer. Accordingly, **the importance of fully developing your RFC issue cannot be overstated.**

This section is only an overview of RFC's, written to make the examiner aware of the issues involved if he or she encounters one on the examination of a used auto dealer. Contact your district ISP for further guidance and updates on the topic.

Made in the USA
San Bernardino, CA
11 June 2019